HOW TO CREATE
FICTIONAL
CHARACTERS

Writers' Bookshop

Writers' Bookshop

HOW TO CREATE FICTIONAL CHARACTERS

JEAN SAUNDERS

CONTENTS

CHAPTER 1

FIRST
THINGS
FIRST

CHARACTER OR SETTING
HUMAN INTEREST
WHAT'S IN A NAME?
MATCHING UP NAMES
DIFFERENTIATING BETWEEN NAMES

CHAPTER 1

CHARACTER OR SETTING

Characters are the life blood of any fiction, and without them a writer might just as well be writing a factual account. But creating fictional characters that leap straight off the page and into the reader's imagination is probably the hardest thing for the new writer to do. It's easy enough to decide to set your short story or novel against an exciting backdrop of wars, intrigue, science fiction or whatever setting takes your fancy. But you still have to people those novels with characters, who seem so alive to the reader that she feels she knows them as real people. (In referring to the reader as 'she', I don't mean to be sexist. I'm simply saving both of us, author and reader, the irritation of constantly using the 'he or she' tag.)

When it comes to the planning stage of any fiction, I consider that there are two distinct types of author. One is the kind who writes directly from character, and who thinks of the characters first and foremost. The storyline in which these characters are going to move develops directly from this character definition.

The other kind of author is the one who finds a background and period in which she is passionately interested. This may be anything from a lethargic summer scene in an English village, to the filth and degradation of the battlefields in the First World War. A background found, the author then decides what sort of characters would logically fit into it.

Neither method is wrong, and nor is one any better than the other. They are merely alternative ways of approaching fiction, and I myself have used both. If I have thought up a really good beginning to a story involving a scintillating piece of dialogue between two strong characters, I have even plunged straight into writing up the scene, and only later stopped to see where the story would lead me from that point. Character is definitely uppermost in this case, and takes charge of the plot.

Plunging right in without planning is not necessarily to be strongly recommended to the absolute beginner. Even so, I have always advocated that no one knows whether or not they can write until they sit down and begin, so it may suit one author far better than another. 'Just beginning' and seeing where your characterisation leads you may be the trigger you need to get you started. And getting started is one of the biggest bugbears to any author, beginner or not.

But the marvellous thing about any kind of writing is the choices you have. Without meaning to sound blasphemous, you can play God for as long as you wish. The characters you create exist solely in your head until you set them down on paper. They are there to be juggled with, loved, victimised, mugged, shamed, exalted, or whatever you care to do with them.

The entire range of human emotions can run through the pages of your novel, but however dramatic your prose may be, those emotions are at their most effective when seen through the eyes of your characters. It's their story, and you are merely the narrator, seeing the story through their eyes and telling it through their voices. Remember your place!

HUMAN INTEREST

It should already be obvious that the characters form the central core of any piece of fiction. Without them to enliven the pages, to walk and talk and breathe through your story, you have only an essay or a descriptive piece to offer your readers. You might as well be writing a crisp journalistic account.

But although this book is devoted to fictional characters for novel and short-story writing, think for a moment about the most poignant journalistic accounts in any newspaper - the one you read at the breakfast table this morning, perhaps. Weren't the most eye-catching stories those with human interest?

I can guarantee that there were stories about at least one of the following: a foreign or domestic disaster; a battle with the tax inspector; trouble at one of Her Majesty's prisons; a famine; a background on a sporting personality; a 'royal' story; a government crisis; a show-biz personality story; the rise or fall of a football hero; the death of a 'personality'; some controversy over schools, the health service, local planning, the railways ...

And none of those stories would catch the attention of the reading public without some detailed reference to at least one named person. Every photograph would focus on a person mentioned in the news story. And in every one, the people most closely involved would be named, their ages given (the media seems obsessed with people's ages), their status in life, their attitudes to other people and/or to the authority mentioned, however briefly.

Anyone, especially those 'of a certain age', standing up for their rights against all the odds, however ill informed and doomed to failure, would be given the status of local hero. Verbal quotes would be included wherever possible. At the very least, there would be reputedly accurate comments 'as told to our correspondent'.

Without such intimate detail to bring those people concerned vividly to life for the reader, such pieces would be flat and far less interesting. We all share a natural human curiosity about other people's lives, however much we may loftily deny it.

And, let's face it, a statement about the resolving of a military crisis is far more immediate and accessible to our imagination when the commander is named and described and quoted, especially when he has larger-than-life qualities that make him stand out against all the rest. Everyone loves a hero.

It's because of this vicarious interest in the lives and doings of these people that we read on. We share in their triumphs. We grieve for their sorrows. We're indignant on their behalf when we feel the judicial system is blind and stupid.

These reactions are exactly the same ones we have where we read any good fiction. The reader is initially curious about the as yet unknown characters in a story, and she opens a novel or a magazine with a feeling of anticipation. She wants to be able to identify with the people she'll be reading about, to share their problems and conflicts and dangers, and to be thankful when they reach their happy or satisfying ending relatively unscathed. Since you and I are both readers, I know you'll agree with me on that point.

She also wants mentally to hiss with the villain, the way they did in the golden days of the silent cinema. In other words, she needs to play a definite part in the entity that is the story. To involve her very early on by her interest in the characters is to keep her involved throughout the rest of the book. In this way, I believe there's a definite relationship between author, characters and reader. It may be a fleeting relationship that ends as soon as the last page of the book is reached, but it exists, and it is strong.

WHAT'S IN A NAME?

The first thing I consider before I even begin to flesh out my characters, is their names. Just as we spend a vast amount of time thinking up a name for a new baby in real life, so we should consider the suitability of our fictional babies' names. As well as finding a name that you as the author are comfortable with, you should think of the impact the name is going to have on the character herself.

Will she be charmed by the unusual name of Tansy, or will she absolutely hate it? Will the Elvis of the 1990s be ridiculed by his classmates, or will he preen himself on his parents' choice and want to follow in the footsteps of his/their idol? Did he even adopt the name himself, rather than the conventional name of Harold or Joe with which he was baptised? Or is your Elvis a middle-aged man, still yearning for the days of the greased DA haircut and winkle-pickers?

If you decide to use either Tansy or Elvis in a short story, contemporary romance, children's book or a teenage novel, for instance, you could use any of the brief comments I've outlined, both as the basis for conflict and to define their characters in various ways, and you could think up other ways of making use of their names.

Everything you say about a character in a story should tell the reader something more about that person, and what better way to start than by the name you choose?

You might think that Tansy lends itself to fey kind of child, or a maid; or perhaps it is the fanciful name given to a child by a doting parent, when her sisters are called by the more prosaic Jane and Mary.

This, in turn, can lead you to consider whether Jane and Mary would be indulgent towards this privileged child, or a bit peeved, or mocking, or downright vindictive at this favouritism. By stretching your own imagination you can see how the combination of the names you give your characters can further the conflict created in your story.

It's important for an author to get a feel for names. For purely practical reasons, you'd hardly call a male character in a historical novel Wayne. Such an anachronism would kill all the authenticity of the rest of your wonderful research - although there are many names that have stood the test of time and will transpose into historical or contemporary fiction.

For characters in historical fiction, authors generally go for longer and more stately names than those they give their modern counterparts, particularly for characters of a higher class. This also applies to everyday names that can be shortened. William is more authoritative than Bill, although the latter is far more friendly. Billy conjures up the name of a child, or a bit of a rogue, or perhaps one who can't quite rid himself of the tag and is perhaps still somewhat tied to the umbilical cord. Again, this is an implication to be exploited in your character definition. Although the final choice of names remains the author's preference, I think it's worth trying to gauge the impact of certain names on the majority of readers.

If you were to name a character Elizabeth, you have the diminutives of Liza, Betty or Beth to play with, any of which would be fine for a historical lady's nickname among her intimates. But a twenties housemaid would probably be known by the more downmarket Lizzie and she would have no pretensions to be called Elizabeth.

Biblical names have an authentic ring to them, and are much used in historical novels. Consider Isaac, Aaron or Joseph. Even an elderly gent called Moses wouldn't seem out of place in a historical. Some biblical names are still fashionable, such as Rebecca, Rachel or Sarah, and would fit into any kind of fiction, whether shortened or not.

In contemporary fiction, names such as Tracey, Sharon or Kylie give an immediate image to characters. Television has much to answer for in these cases, but we can't deny its existence or its influence, any more than we can deny that film stars have influenced popular names of a certain era. There are many Marilyns named after Monroe who may or may not live to regret it, though I've yet to meet a Zsa Zsa in real life or fiction.

A useful book to have on your shelf is a book of babies' names. I also recommend *The Guinness Book of Names* by Leslie Dunkling, which gives a huge variety of names from which to choose, including the most popular names at given dates in history, in this country and in others.

Naturally if your character is not English you will have to name her appropriately. It's easy enough to put a Catriona into a Scottish setting; a Bridget in an Irish setting; or a Bronwyn in a Welsh one. But you may want a Norwegian hero or a Slavic one, and this is where those foreign films on television are useful. They list plenty of foreign names in the credits, and providing you can be sure which are male and which are female, you can start devising your own lists.

Among other reference books on my shelves, I have the *Collins Gem Thesaurus of Synonyms and Antonyms*. It's a small book and no real rival to *Roget's Thesaurus*, but as well as other snippets of information it contains an A to Z of Christian names in English with their equivalents in Latin, French, Italian, Spanish and German. I've found this useful on numerous occasions, and it has saved a lot of further searching.

Some of the variations are slight, but it always gives me enormous satisfaction to get it right. For example, Christopher is Christophorus (L); Christophe (F); Christoforo (I); Christobal (S); Christoph (G). Bridget is Brigitta (L); Brigitte (F); Brigida (I); Brigida (S); Brigitte (G). Edward is Eduardus (L); Edouard (F); Eduardo (I); Eduardo (S); Eduard (G). Frederick is Fredericus (L); Frederic (F); Federico (I); Federico (S); Friedrich or Fritz (G). John is Jo(h)annes (L); Jean (F); Giovanni (I); Juan (S); Johann (G).

MATCHING UP NAMES

You should remember to match your characters' names, not only to their nationalities but to their status in life, and to their times. Shortened versions of popular names became fashionable in Victorian times, but in the twenties era of the flappers there was also a great vogue for female nicknames such as Bunty and Fliss. If you match your characters' names to their personalities, the reader will form an instant impression of what a girl called Prissy might be like, even before she's learned anything more about her. This could be a bit of a tease, because Prissy could be simply a nickname for Priscilla, or could be a description of a fusspot. In one of my books she was the former, and she appeared in my Masquerade historical, *Outback Woman* by Sally Blake, and it was useful for other characters to remark how unlike she was to her own fussy nickname.

Match your characters' forenames to their prospective partners and associates in the story, and to their surnames. You don't want your characters' names to jar on the reader. Remember, your reader is (with luck) assuming that these people you've created are real, so don't label a character with something impossible to read or pronounce, in which case the reader will skip the name every time she sees it in the story. Avoid labelling your people with something so gimmicky that it sounds ridiculous.

Jewel names for female characters are attractive, providing they suit the book you're writing. Name your heroine Jade or Pearl or Sapphire or Beryl and readers will see her as one of four distinct types. Many of these names overlap with the colours. A girl called Amber once evoked a very special image in fiction, and Scarlett surely needs no explanation. Red suits a redhead or a fiery hero; Skye is delicate and Chalky White - how many times have we met him in fiction!

Flower names automatically compare the character with the flower she represents. Daisy sounds light and fresh; Jasmine exotic; Primrose perhaps a little prim; Rose and her variations can be anything you want her to be; Daphne, Myrtle or Marigold have their own appeal, and almost lend their descriptions to you, both by their sounds and their familiar botanical appearance and fragrances. Holly might be a little prickly; Poppy's bright and young; Hazel sounds gentle.

I get many of my surnames from the street names where I live, and in any town I visit. It's far more interesting than simply going through the telephone book, which is another obvious alternative. By now I've become quite a collector of names, and I warn you that this kind of simple research can become pleasantly addictive and take you away from the real business of writing. But since it's important to feel you have both forenames and surnames of your characters absolutely right, I think it's time well spent. And if you keep a special notebook for the purpose, you will have your own ready-made supply of names that appeal particularly to you when you next have some interesting characters to name in a new story.

DIFFERENTIATING BETWEEN NAMES

Letting your readers see the characters clearly by the names you give them is an art in itself. It's often best to avoid the alliteration of having forenames and surnames beginning with the same letter. Yet there is arguably a certain flow about it, and sometimes it can even add to the interpretation of the character. Naming a character Dolly Dilkes in my book *The Bannister Girls* is an example in point. Dolly Dilkes was a pert, young, brash Cockney, and I felt that her alliterative names slid off the tongue to give exactly the impression I wanted. There was even a slight hint of Cockney dialect/implied slang in its euphemism with jellied eel ... but perhaps that's taking fancy a little *too* far.

Pretty little Polly Perkins is another fictional character where the matching letters of fore and surnames fit comfortably. If you use them together, let them make a point. But be careful when giving your attractive contemporary heroine the name of Holly that your hero's surname isn't Berry ... the euphony here is more inclined to make the reader ridicule the end result than admire it. Such points are so obvious, but how often do we forget something like this, that would necessitate going back through the entire book to change one of the names when the couple get married in the final chapter?

Date-related names are interesting, and can usefully be employed in fiction to underline a period. Could Poppy's surge in popularity have come from the First World War era and the Flanders poppy? Did a clutch of little Evas emerge because of Eva Peron? Doris Day undoubtedly made a rather dull name livelier because of her own movie image - and an alliterative name certainly didn't do her any harm!

Royal forenames inevitably produce their clones and are inclined to date-stamp their owners; this can usefully be employed in fiction. Albert comes from the Prince Consort; Diana from the former Princess of Wales, no doubt Beatrice will be the in name for the teenagers of a few years hence.

Despite the aura surrounding such men of stature as Winston Churchill, the name has rarely caught on as a forename except in ethnic communities. And few British parents would be daring enough to call their sons Adolph, for obvious reasons. In Spanish communities, Jesus is a common name; yet it is never seen here. All of these names could sensibly have a place in fiction, but because of their associations, all would have pre-conceived attributes accorded to them by the reader, whether consciously or sub-consciously.

There's an odd theory that the letter M is used more often in creating fictional characters than any other. I have no explanation for this, but since it's one of the middle letters of the alphabet, perhaps an author is more drawn to it than any other for some inexplicable reason. But wasn't James Bond's chief and mentor called simply M? To say nothing of Miss Moneypenny... I tested out this strange theory for myself, by looking back through my own novels, and was quite startled to find how many M characters I've used. I discovered that I've used Morwen, Matt, Matthew, Marc, Mark, Maxwell, Margot, Miranda, Marina, Michael, Mick, Marnie, Margaret, Meg, Marianne, Margaretta, Mel, Meera, Monty, Madelyn ... Surnnames have been Montalban, McKuen, Mackenzie, Mackinnon, Mackinty, Morrow, McConnell, Mitchell, Merrick, Morland, Montagu ... It's a little eerie when you start checking up. Perhaps there's something in the mystique of the M letter after all. Or perhaps it's simply an unconscious favourite of mine, and of other authors too.

But it's a very good idea to keep a tally of all the names you use in your stories, especially those with large casts, to ensure that your favourite doesn't occur too often. And of course, the M names I quoted above were liberally distributed throughout my books, and didn't all occur in the same one!

One thing I'm careful to do is to avoid giving two of my characters similar-sounding names. I wouldn't normally have two characters with the same forename in the same book, unless it was for a special reason; and then only if one of them regularly used a distinctive nickname. Nothing irritates a reader more than to have to check back to see who is who.

In one of my recent novels, the hero's name is Vincent Montagu. I deliberately gave his grandfather the same name in order to provide an identity mix-up. But once it's established that the older man has always been known as Monty (those M letters again), the two men are kept quite separate in both the heroine's and the reader's mind.

I'm also conscious of choosing names that begin with varying letters of the alphabet. This is easy enough in a short story or short novel, but with a large cast, it can get a little difficult. Again, my checklist comes into play; each time a new character comes into the story I jot down his or her name, and keep a running check of the names, their sounds and their initial letters.

I don't think time spent deciding on the names of your fictional characters is time wasted. I'm willing to bet that any parent spends weeks and months of deliberation before finding exactly the right name for their own flesh and blood baby, and, during this time, they will discard many ideas along the way. I don't suggest you spend *that* long; your story will never get written. But if you intend to be a dedicated author with a real understanding of what makes your characters tick, you'll feel that same sense of duty over the names you choose for them, and will want to get them exactly right.

You will have to decide whether or not there could ever be another Scarlett, or if there is a case for your Victoria being known as Vicki, or if your quaint-sounding Loveday was right for a West Country regional novel. It sounded perfect to me when I named my own Loveday Willard in my historical novel *The Sweet Red Earth* by Rowena Summers, set in and around the Somerset cider-apple orchards. And yes, I chose that pen name too, when I felt I needed another identity for my books. It seemed to fit the new kind of novels I was then writing. But, believe me, even choosing different pen names can take a deal of thought and discarding of the unlikely, because if readers take to an author, and the books start to get a following, she's going to be stuck with that new name. And that's a delightful prospect - providing you're not going to be labelled something like Nellie Bloggs for the foreseeable future.

There's more to authorship than gazing into space and chewing the end of a pen awaiting the so-called muse, or sitting in front of a typewriter or word processor and thinking that the words will come without any conscious effort, than the novice ever imagines.

But that's the biggest myth of all, and I never knew the muse yet that couldn't be helped along by all the hard work that goes into producing a story that excites or intrigues the reader, who puts down the book with a satisfied sigh of pleasure. And the process all begins with the characters ...

CHAPTER 2

VOICES AND DIALOGUE

THE CHARACTER'S VOICE
ACCENTS AND DIALECT
ADVERBS TO QUALIFY 'HE SAID'
LISTEN TO REAL (AND TV) VOICES

CHAPTER 2

Once you've settled on the names for your characters, thought out a storyline in which they will move and behave and decided to begin the actual writing, you'll begin to face the problem of dialogue. This is the area in fiction that frightens beginners most. If it doesn't frighten them, they often find they don't have the remotest idea of the purpose behind fictional dialogue, and unless they learn some of the techniques, nothing in their manuscript will work.

We all know that dialogue consists of conversation between people. In real life, it consists of many trite and inconsequential asides, broken sentences and day-to-day trivia. But in fiction, there's no room for meaningless trivia. I qualify the word, because certain trivia in fiction is perfectly valid and may be there to show something of the nature of the person speaking. Even a character who habitually speaks in the sort of clichés that you would never use in the narrative has his value, because those speech patterns help to underline the person he is.

All the words you put into your characters' mouths must be thought out carefully, and then written as if it was the most natural thing in the world for those people to say to one another at that given point. It sounds easy. Very often, it's not.

The purpose of fictional dialogue is complex. It defines character. It moves the story forward. It reveals something of a character's past, his present actions and future hopes. It explains in a smooth and easily assimilated form what the author wants the reader to know. It brings the characters to life more effectively than anything else in the story. Most basically of all, it relieves the eye from too much plain narrative, varying the look of the page and bringing people into what would otherwise be no more than an essay. But it also allows the reader to eavesdrop on all those delicious conversations we may dearly like to hear in real life, and cannot, or dare not. It lets us take a vicarious interest in other people's lives while we read of their stories through the pages of a short story or novel.

THE CHARACTER'S VOICE

Because of the importance of dialogue to every character, the very first thing I do when I've settled on my character's name is to give her a voice. Each of us has a voice as individual to us as our fingerprints, and so should your fictional characters. The voice can be soft or strident, infuriatingly slow-speaking, or rapid Cockney; regional, foreign, slurred by drink or illness, wavering, melodic, shrill or gruff ... again, the choices are infinite. Whatever your choice, stick with it and identify your character in your own mind by the voice you've given her. Every time you let her speak her lines of dialogue, listen to that voice in your head saying those words. Once you get into the habit of doing that, the inflexion will be right; the choice of words the character uses will be right; the mood and the actual speech patterns will be right. What's more, you won't forget halfway through the story what impression you were trying to put across to your reader, and change her personality completely without realising it, because she'll be in effect 'telling' you she wouldn't speak that way ...

ACCENTS AND DIALECT

It's obviously useful for your regionally-based heroine to have the accent they will immediately identify as living in Cornwall or Scotland or Yorkshire or Ireland. If you set your story in those areas, it's comfortable and obvious to have a heroine who speaks the same language as everyone else.

But sometimes you want her to be out of her own environment, and the simple fact of placing a Yorkshire lass in a Cornish fishing village, for example, can create a whole lot of problems for her that you hadn't envisaged. Using such a simple trick in order to further the conflict in the story will stretch your imagination as a writer. Local folk often don't take kindly to outsiders, particularly those living in insular or remote areas. For the hero - or villain - to discover quite suddenly that the girl he's been stalking from afar, is someone who sounds completely different from his expectations can create entirely new scenes, and perhaps move your story in different directions from the one the reader has been expecting.

The impact of the character's voice shouldn't be under-estimated in fiction. How she talks on the telephone, happiness or pain, to a variety of different people, or in any given situation, can influence your reader's opinion enormously.

Imagine for a moment a heroine, whom we'll call Louise. In your imagination, give her a child to comfort, or an elderly lady to care for. Give her a burglar to confront, or an unpleasant business underling to deal with, or a lover to greet on returning home from a war ... and give her some words to say.

In every case, the words would be different. The voice may be rushed or hurried or compassionate, scared or husky or embarrassed ... but it would be the same voice, acting out different situations with different people. And this is an important point to remember. Although the voice you've given her will be the same, the way your character uses it will vary according to the person she's speaking to. After all, we don't speak in the same tones to the vicar and the milkman or to our spouse and the irritating kid next door!

What your character says, and how she says it, can make or break her credibility with your reader. It's perilously easy to write awful dialogue that has the characters saying virtually nothing of interest. In a short story particularly, where every word must count, there's simply no room for wasteful dialogue. And in a novel, your characters would soon lose credibility if they just waffled on and on.

The following examples show the difference between good and bad dialogue between two characters.

```
1.
'Why don't we go to the pictures?' Ruth said.
'What's on, Ruth?' Angela answered.
'I don't know, Angela. Shall I find out?'
'Where's the paper? I don't believe I've seen it
today.'
'It's on the kitchen table, I think, Angela,' Ruth
said.
'I'll get it then, shall I, Ruth?'
'Yes please, Angela.'
```

> **2.**
> 'So why don't we go to the pictures tonight?' Ruth said impatiently.
> Angela shrugged. 'Oh, if you like. Is there anything worth seeing? I haven't even looked at the local paper yet.'
> 'I'll take a look and then we can decide if it's worth moving away from the fire,' Ruth said, yawning.

No prizes for guessing which example is the better one. This is only a tiny scene in a story, but in the first one (which admittedly is blatantly contrived to be bad) the dialogue is jerky and forced. It's totally unnecessary to mention both characters' names in every sentence. The detail the reader needs to know is trivialised, both by the staccato sentences and by the resulting block of indented dialogue on the printed page.

While it's quite correct to indent every new line of dialogue to identify who's speaking, I feel you should also pay attention to the aesthetic look of the page as well as to the flow of the words. Try to visualise the condensed printed page as well as your own handwritten rough or your neatly typed or word-processed pages.

The second scene above is seemingly much briefer, but in fact, has exactly the same number of words. The information is conveyed much more smoothly; here are two girls, somewhat bored and too lazy to move away from the fire (suggesting that this is a winter evening), deciding what to do with themselves. There's no need to define who is speaking in each case. The careful use of words such as 'impatiently' and 'shrugged', and the description of Ruth yawning, are enough to set the tone of the whole scene.

An example of a war scene is given next. Although the writing is fluent, in the first scene the entire dramatic effect is lost because of the dialogue.

1.

It seemed as if they had been in the air in their flimsy plane for hours, but at last the battle was almost over. The relief showed on their faces, and Tom spoke cheerfully to his gunner.

'I'll be glad when we get back home after this little lot, Jimmy. It'll be roast beef and Yorkshire pudding at the mother-in-law's for Sunday dinner, and forget all about looking for the Hun for a while.'

'You and your Sunday dinner! It's a wonder you can fit into the cockpit, the amount you eat. Your wife deserves a medal for feeding you up the way she does.'

'Look out, here comes another of the blighters, straight out of the sun as usual, the crafty devils. Get him, Jimmy!'

2.

It seemed as if their flimsy plane had been in the air for hours, but at last the battle was almost over. Relief showed on their grimed faces, but Tom still spoke warily to his gunner.

'Nearly there, mate! What do you say to a pint at the local when we get back to Blighty -?'

He swore beneath his breath as a flash of silver came straight towards them out of the sun. The Hun was still on their tail, and he wasn't done with them yet.

'You'd better save any thoughts of that pint until we've finished with this little lot!' the gunner yelled back. 'Give me all the speed you've got, Skipper.'

The difference in these two scenes lies in the way the dialogue in the first holds up the sense of action and tension. Discussing mundane matters at such length becomes tedious, and the references to the enemy as 'crafty devils' is weak dialogue.

In this case too, Tom's comments that the enemy is coming straight out of the sun as usual is contrived for the reader's benefit, since his gunner would know this fact only too well. The information is better given as straight prose as in the second example.

In this scene, the action moves at a far brisker pace. The reader is aware of the tension, relieved briefly by the thought of a pint at the local, but quickly reinstated, both by the pilot's oath and by the need to get out of there fast, as spoken by his gunner. Here too, Tom spoke warily, giving the reader a hint that the worst wasn't yet over; in the first example he spoke cheerfully, destroying the sense of drama.

These two scenes are only minimally different, but the reader's reaction to them would be vastly different, both because of the words the characters use, and the implied tone of their voices. In the first, Tom is breezing along, seemingly unaware of the danger still surrounding them, and Jimmy is indulging him. They're schoolboys, playing at war.

In the second, he's a responsible pilot, tense and battle-fatigued, and drawing the reader directly into his world. Jimmy isn't named at this point, but called 'mate'. This simplifies their relationship, and also defines their status, as does Jimmy's use of the word 'Skipper'.

ADVERBS TO QUALIFY 'HE SAID'

Using dialogue in fiction serves several purposes. Of course you need to hear your characters speak, if only to break up the pages of prose and relieve the reader from reading what might just as well be a text book. But dialogue helps to define character more than anything else, as do those qualifying adverbs you use after the quotation marks.

Some tutors will say no adverbs are ever needed, and that the strength of the dialogue alone will say all that's needed. This is not totally true. Certainly, you can let the reader see whether a character is ponderous by the unending, weighty sentences he speaks.

You can reveal fear and tension in speech in short, terse sentences, but there are times when that little extra word can give just the exact meaning you want to portray. In my opinion, it's as foolish to forget adverbs altogether as to say you must delete every bit of description from your story. If you pare it down too much, you'll have nothing left.

The stark sentence that follows could quite well stand alone in any story.

```
'You don't love me anymore,' Kate said.
```

Think how the impact of this sentence is changed if Kate says the words slowly, tearfully, furiously or passionately. You can elaborate further by ending the sentence fully and then extending the qualifying phrase.

```
   'You don't love me anymore.' Kate was filled with
disbelief.
   'You don't love me anymore.' Kate almost spat the words
at him.
```

In each of these cases, you sense a different Kate, a different mood. With little more to go on, you almost sense the scene that's taking place. You also sense the reaction of the second character, before and after Kate has spoken. You could alter the impact of this one line of dialogue still more in the following ways.

```
   'You - don't love me anymore?' Kate said hoarsely.
   'You don't love me anymore!' Kate screamed.
   'You don't love me anymore,' Kate said, sadly.
```

It's your choice. Putting the emphasis on certain words, the use of adverbs, and selected punctuation marks can all accentuate the way you want to present your character to the reader in a certain mood.

If you have great difficulty putting your characters' dialogue into your mouths, then try saying it aloud as you write. Put all the anger, passion, fear, sorrow into the words as if your character was saying them. You may find this embarrassing at first, and it's obviously best done in private. But it's the best way of learning how a character would speak, which words are impossible for him to say, and those that are awkward for the reader to read.

LISTEN TO REAL (AND TV) VOICES

Relating voices to real people is a useful trick when 'listening' to your own characters. Someone you've seen many times on television, such as a newscaster, perhaps listen to the nasal tones of Sandy Gall, or the smooth ones of Alistair Burnet. Or how about one of those Australian soaps for a quick low-down on the Aussie accent, to say nothing of the current idioms in use, whether you like them or not. To get authenticity in your characters, you have to swallow your own prejudices and really get inside the skins - and the heads - of your characters.

An autocratic lady could perhaps speak *à la* Margaret Thatcher; and a plausible cad like the character Peter Bowles plays in *Perfect Scoundrels*. Studying people on television is a quick and easy way of seeing how actors and politicians portray the impression they want by the varying inflexions of their voices.

The chances are that everyone has someone in their family whose voice and speech patterns they've sometimes longed to mimic - an elderly aunt, perhaps, still living in the past and never letting you forget it. Or a fusspot of a grandfather, who insists on smoking his pipe and fouling the air, and telling everyone loudly that smoking never did him any harm, and he'll be 92 in January ... a twittering younger sister, boring you to death by her endless recitals about the latest boyfriend ... These are your ready-made prototypes. Draw on them and exaggerate them, but for Heaven's sake don't name them as your relatives unless you want a libel suit on your hands! Very few real people recognise themselves in fiction. If they do, they invariably think of themselves as the goodies, and never as the villains. But it pays to be careful all the same. What usually happens is that you end up making a pot-pourri of real people's characteristics - a little of Aunt Joan, a bit of cousin Lesley, a touch of that irritating woman across the way ...

Give your fictional characters some of the wonderful conversational traits you can discover all around you by listening on the bus, in a cinema queue, at a wedding, or even something as terrible as witnessing a road accident. It may sound in very poor taste to mention such an emotional time as being the source of character study, but the true writer is hardly conscious of researching into the emotions. Somehow you almost become two people at such times. One of you is giving all the comfort and sympathy that may be needed; the other is registering everything that's going on in little cameo scenes to be recalled at some later date when you want to remember exactly how it felt, and to transfer all that emotion to your characters.

The last thing you want an editor to say about your dialogue is that it is wooden or stilted, and only by reading through your work and revising it until it flows properly should you be satisfied with it. Always ask yourself if it's feasible that your character should say the things that she does. Is it true to her character? Is it true to her background?

Imagine you have an American GI chatting up a pretty girl from a Somerset village during the Second World War. He's unlikely to approach her in the same way an English Tommy would, and her response is likely to be very different. He may be brash. He may be ill at ease at being in a different environment and thousands of miles away from home. She may be nervous, flattered, hoping desperately that her friends will see her, and that her parents will not. All these things will have an effect on the way they regard one another, but their basic speech patterns will be true to their natures and backgrounds.

```
    'Hi there, honey. Say, didn't I see you with your
girlfriend at the village hop last night?'
    Josie tilted her head to look at the good-looking
Yank.
    'That depends if you were looking. I'm usually there on
a Saturday night.'
    'Is that so? Then maybe I'll see you there next week.
Is it a date?'
    'Cheeky, aren't you? I don't make dates with blokes I
don't know -'she began.
    'Well, that's easily taken care of. The name's Hank. So
let me guess what they call you. Candy, or Cindy?'
    She gave a nervous laugh. 'Now you're making fun of me.
The name's Josie Green, not something daft and made up
like one of them blooming film stars.'
    'No kidding. Well, I'm telling you that from where I'm
looking, Josie Green could surely be in the movies, honey,'
Hank said easily.
```

This small scene of dialogue encapsulates the characters of two people as briefly as possible. You don't need to be told that Hank's throwing her a line, and that Josie's going to fall for it. You're already feeling some sympathy for Josie, and a bit of grudging admiration for the rogue that Hank will probably turn out to be.

Or maybe you're not. Maybe you think Josie sounds a silly little idiot, but that Hank could really have a foot in the door of the movie industry and could do great things for her if she doesn't let the opportunity go. The important thing is that those few lines of dialogue would get you curious. You'd want to read on to see what happened next.

Note in particular the general absence of 'he saids' and 'she saids'. There's no need to qualify every line of dialogue, especially when the conversation is between two such diverse characters, where each identity is immediately obvious to the reader. It needs to be used occasionally, even in this short piece of work, if only to prevent the ping-pong look of the page. This also illustrates how using the right adverb can go a long way to persuading the reader into your frame of mind. In the last sentence, I used 'Hank said easily' quite deliberately. That one word 'easily' suggests a pretty smooth character, and one who means to take every advantage of our poor country girl. What comes next would be up to every individual author.

Again, be careful with dialect. It can be difficult to read and it will slow down the flow of the story while a reader tries to work out the regional variations you've used for authenticity. Very often, just the flavour of a regional patois is all that's necessary. The GI's use of the word 'honey' and his general speech rhythms define him perfectly well, as do Josie's more down-to-earth use of 'daft' and her phrase 'one of them blooming film stars'.

The many variations of 'he said', 'she said', can be infuriatingly difficult to sort out for the beginning writer. Sometimes those two simple words are all that's needed, and pass almost unnoticed in the text when you're reading it. Extremes such as 'he expostulated', 'riposted', 'extrapolated' and so on, are cumbersome and only to be used occasionally, if at all. Active verbs, such as 'she screamed', 'yelled', 'sobbed', 'wept', 'joked', etc are useful terms to use, but, again, only in moderation.

If you use earthy characters in your stories, you must be prepared to give them earthy dialogue. A lout being caught by the police just as he's about to fall into the getaway car isn't going to react by using the

Queen's English. A Yorkshire hill farmer preparing for a day working his sheep would be likely to say, 'I'll not be back for my dinner while sevenish, lass.'

Be true to your characters and let them be true to themselves in their speech. And as a final test, try tuning into any favourite TV programme, and then turning off the sound. Would *The Darling Buds of May* ever be the same without hearing the wonderfully spivvy asides of David Jason as Pop. They are as true to the essence of HE Bates' character as any could be, but we grew to know them even more when a voice was added to them.

Remember *Dynasty*, and the contrast of Joan Collins' plummy Alexis and the husky tones of Krystle? If you hadn't known the actresses concerned, wouldn't you have been surprised and intrigued once you turned on the sound? That incredibly *English* voice among all those Americans ... what was she doing there, and how did she come to marry Blake Carrington? (We shall probably never know ...)

Conversely, in a radio play, you have only the sounds of the different voices to rely on, and every emotion has to be conveyed through the nuance of the voice. This subtle blend of inflexion and speech pattern should be as vivid for your readers through the words you write on the page, such is the power of voice and dialogue to a character. Always be aware of it when you're creating yours.

CHAPTER 3

HEROES AND HEROINES

LARGER-THAN-LIFE HEROES
DESCRIBING YOUR HERO
TODAY'S HEROINES
A CHARACTER CHECKLIST

CHAPTER 3

In my opinion, most novels of whatever genre benefit from having some kind of love interest, or, at the very least, some ongoing conflict between a man and a woman, even if it's not resolved at the end. Conflict is what makes fiction readable, so no story should be so bland, and no characters all so loveable and squeaky clean that the reader is bored before she's read halfway down the first few pages.

A fictional hero does not only have to be the one mythically beloved of romantic novelists (in whose ranks I count myself), that tall, dark and handsome creature of impossibly arrogant manners who will sometimes come and sweep the poor little heroine off her feet and away into the fictional sunset ... If that is what you believe of current romantic heroes, then where have you been for the last decade? Heroes in romantic fiction have become far more realistic and believable than they were in some of the early books that got the genre a bad name. But don't totally blame the authors. In the thirties and forties and even very recently, readers were far less sophisticated than they are now, and that type of hero was just what readers craved.

Enter Rhett Butler. Yes, the cinema has much to answer for in the way every woman expected her hero to be of that tall, dark and handsome variety, and was so let down when she found her ordinary, be-slippered, cuddly bear of a partner was so much less ... No wonder, then, that she was dazzled by fiction, and astute publishers signed up authors prepared to give her just the excitement she craved.

LARGER-THAN-LIFE HEROES

But to be practical, the fictional hero does have to be larger than life. He is invariably tall in a romance, but not necessary so in other genres. The exception is obviously James Bond, whom no reader in her right mind could call anything but the archetypal romantic dare-devil hero, even though these books certainly couldn't be categorised as romantic. In so many cases, though, the genres overlap, despite the frantic wishes of publishers and booksellers to keep them all in neat little compartments.

But what of Hercule Poirot, who was surely Agatha Christie's most unlikely creation, but a hero no less? Fastidious to the point of irritating fussiness, small, foreign (at least to British readers), so irritatingly and inevitably always proved right ... Could any woman ever ally herself to that man? Yet he still comes over as the undoubted champion in the novels, and most of the female characters in the books are clearly fascinated by him.

Ruth Rendell's Inspector Wexford is little more than a country policeman, bluff, not always considerate towards his wife, and certainly often intolerant of his sidekick. But still we love him. And who can deny the appeal of HE Bates' gorgeous old rogue of a hero, Pop Larkin? I'd read him and loved him long before the television screen and David Jason took him over, but he's surely not what the media hype would have you believe is a regular hero. So perhaps it's all in the mind of the reader, and more importantly, in the words of the writer, how we come to regard the men in the fiction we read. We love Pop Larkin because he's certainly no country bumpkin. He's smart enough always to be one step ahead of authority, but he does it with good humour and without malice. If you write about your hero with that kind of sympathetic understanding, the sympathy will transmit itself to the reader. If you write about him tongue in cheek, when you don't really care about him at all, be assured that this will come through as well.

If heroes do not have to be of a regulation shape and size, they do have to have redeeming qualities in their make-up, otherwise they couldn't be classed as heroes. The hero is the central male character of the book or short story, and as such he must dominate the pages to the extent that all other male characters are subsidiary to him.

You may argue that certain types of detective heroes always have sidekicks that seem just as important. Imagine Sherlock Holmes without his Watson ... when you think of Conan Doyle's books, you may not separate the two of them in your mind, yet you are in no doubt which is the dominant character. When James Herriott created his alter ego for his series of books about a country vet, he created an entire locality of interesting characters; but James still stands the tallest among them all.

DESCRIBING YOUR HERO

Creating your hero out of your imagination is obviously the easiest and best way to go about it, but some people have great difficulty in starting off the imaginative process. If you get stuck, think of your favourite TV or movie heroes: Nigel Havers, Kevin Kline, Tom Cruise, Michael Keaton, Robert Redford, Tom Selleck, Woody Allen if you must. Model your heroes on the attributes of your favourites. Pin photographs of them in front of you as you write, to remember what attracted you to them, and to help you transfer that attraction on to paper as you create your own fictional hero.

Draw on the character traits of the best fictional heroes of past novelists, the Heathcliffs, Rochesters, Darcys ... but if you do this, use their auras only as starting points to create your own original characters, and don't start rewriting *Wuthering Heights, Jane Eyre* or *Pride and Prejudice*. Plagiarism is always a danger if you follow someone else's writing too closely, even in the mere descriptions of gallant heroes. And aside from being unethical and extremely foolish, who wants to be a carbon copy of someone else?

Be original in your writing, while getting all the help you can from these outside sources. It's no disgrace to have some help from photographs and pictures. Some magazine editors used to send out photos to their regular writers around which to build a story, and some publishers do the same thing today; there's no reason to think you're doing something underhand by using some methods.

Illustrated below are a few of the ways I've described some of my own fictional heroes.

```
    Normally he was understanding, but now he gave a superior
sigh. I remember wondering right then why it was that
men changed like chameleons when it came to their cars.
I reckon they resemble them too, the way they say dogs
and their owners grow to look alike. The sports car was
strong and powerful, like Terry himself. It also had the
same short fuse. (From The First Lesson, a short story
originally in Woman.)
```

> A strong male voice with a faint Scots burr spoke right beside her. Sarah spun round to stare at the tall, powerfully built man, a red kerchief tied round his head, and another like a cummerbund around his waist. He wore a loose-fitting shirt and leather trousers, and he looked down at her as if he owned the world and everything in it.
>
> Sarah took in his garb in an instant, but it was the man himself who took her breath away. If this was Black Robbie, and undoubtedly it was, then he was nothing like she had imagined. She had assumed he would be old and ugly and thickset. But this man could be no more than thirty years old, and he was hypnotically handsome, his skin darkly tanned by the hot sun of southern climes.
> (From *Buccaneer's Bride*, historical adventure romance: Jean Innes; Zebra Books, USA).
>
> 'Are you still trying to arrange my life, Ma?' A lazy masculine voice spoke from the doorway, making Rosie jump. She looked up quickly. He seemed to fill the open space of the doorway, and from the darker interior the image of him was dark against light. For a second, Rosie felt her heart thud, and then Will Merrick came further into the room and she saw his face clearly.
>
> He was rugged rather than handsome, but when he smiled the creases on his cheeks and around his eyes made her want to smile back. His eyes were bluer than her own, his jawline strong. Rosie guessed instantly that nobody was going to arrange Will Merrick's life except Will Merrick.
> (From *Willow Harvest*, regional historical: Rowena Summers; Sphere/Severn House).

These examples show various ways of presenting the hero to the reader.

In the first, Terry is compared with a sports car, immediately identifying him with something fast and powerful. This description is much briefer than in those of the novels, since this is from a short story, where every word must count.

In the first of the novel excerpts, the hero is also seen through the heroine's eyes, but the description is more detailed and sensual, and borders on straight description. This is a blatantly sexy hero, bursting in on the heroine's birthday party with all the swashbuckling nerve of the pirate, and quickly evoking to the reader the sense of the adventures that will lie ahead.

In *Willow Harvest*, the hero is again seen through the heroine's eyes, but this is an earthy story with rural characters and a more simplistic way of describing them. In this scene, some of the heroine's own characteristics are also shown when describing the hero.

Such comparisons are subtle and always useful in aiding your descriptions. All of the above are *indirect* descriptions, in that they do not come from the hero himself, or from the author's statements except in the borderline case in *Buccaneer's Bride*.

The following example gives two quite different descriptions of the same man. The first brief description shows how the heroine first sees him and gets an instant impression of the physical appearance of the man. The second part occurs a few pages further on in the book, and is how the hero describes himself and his present circumstances, and lets the reader into his personality.

```
1.
    ... and then she felt her entire nervous system begin
to prickle with stunned disbelief as she looked into the
handsome, elegant features of Albert of Saxe Coburg, the
Prince Consort.
    Just as quickly, Alex(andra) realised that of course it
wasn't the prince. Albert had been her idol ...


2.
    Fraser Mackinnon threw his valise on the cabin bunk,
the blackness of his thoughts descending on him again
like a heavy cloud. For a few minutes on the dockside,
he had managed to forget his depression, but the little
rich lassie and her prim-nosed aunt had been no more than
diversions to Fraser, and now he unfastened his rain
cape and let it slide to the floor without noticing it.
He pushed the valise after it and lay full-length on the
hard, uncomfortable bunk. He put his hands behind his
head and stared unseeingly at the ceiling.
    This last leave home had promised to be a good one, and he
had been looking forward to the breath of the Highlands in
his lungs again. It was still home, for all that he felt this
need to answer the call of the wild, the exotic, whatever it
was that had made him pursue this dream of India, instead
of being merely content to be a Scottish landowner like
his father. (Both extracts from Golden Destiny, historical:
Jean Saunders; Sphere/Severn House.)
```

In *Golden Destiny* (1) when Alex first sees the hero, she is startled by his resemblance to Prince Albert, whose description already occurs earlier in the book, thus sharpening the reader's perception of how the fictional hero looks.

Later, in (2), Fraser Mackinnon is defined by direct description. A considerable amount of information about his appearance and character is contained in these few short paragraphs, so that he becomes very real to the reader from an early stage in the book.

TODAY'S HEROINES

This book is not intended to deal only with characters in romantic fiction, a genre which is dealt with fully in my book *The Craft of Writing Romance* (also available in this series). But inevitably, when speaking of heroes and heroines, the romantics cannot be ignored, if only to define the changes that have occurred in recent years.

The heroine in a romantic novel or short story has moved far away from what was considered the convention. In the old days she used to be a simpering wimp of a girl, awaiting the pleasure of the hero or suffering at the hands of the villain. Either of these males had a rakish side to them, while she was Little Miss Purity. She had little spirit, and not much incentive to do anything for herself.

Times have changed dramatically for her, to the relief of readers and authors alike. She now has a mind of her own. She is a woman of the 21st century, confident and capable, but still essentially feminine. She is a woman with intrinsic values of home and family and fair play. She's perfectly capable of making her career her main goal in life, but also perfectly agreeable to switching her goals entirely when a man capable of sweeping her off her feet comes along.

But this is where the illusion of the old-style romance ends, because the style of today's writing is vastly different. Television has played its part again, even more so than the movies did when we spent a leisurely couple of hours in a darkened cinema and were still captivated by the aura of a vintage drama such as seeing Margaret Lockwood in *The Wicked Lady*. And long after we went home and curled up in our beds, we would be imagining ourselves as the heroine, with the hero's demanding mouth crushing down on ours ... This type of writing may be as outmoded as the film itself, which still has enormous appeal for its nostalgia value. But today's heroines live in a very different world from that of crinolines and cruel taskmasters, and the descriptions of contemporary heroines reflect that image.

Today's young women drive fast cars and run businesses; they may take flying lessons or decide to join an Outward Bound team, scaling mountains or crewing small boats in unchartered seas; they may join a branch of the Forces, seeking adventures in what was always considered a man's world.

And this creates a whole, marvellous, new area for character conflict in fiction, because always remember that however much fashions change, emotions remain the same. People still get hurt, they laugh and sing and make love, they feel jealousy, passion and hate. All these emotions are there to be used to the full in the make-up of your characters, even though the occupations for your heroines has vastly changed.

The destitute heroine in the more closeted world of historical fiction would most likely be employed as a servant. There was little else for her to do unless she resorted to prostitution. The slightly better-off might be a children's nanny, or a paid companion. Class consciousness was impenetrable in those days, and your heroine's position in life would be very much dictated by her wealth or lack of it.

This is a godsend to the historical novelist, but in contemporary fiction class divisions are not so sharply defined. Fashions have become accessible to everyone now, to the extent that you could walk down any high street and find it hard to gauge which of a group of young women was a waitress or a highly paid computer expert, a mechanic or a hairdresser. The cloning that sometimes results from such mass-market fashion designing could be your starting point for a story involving a mix-up in identity.

Heroines in fiction can range from the spirited Cathy Earnshaw in *Wuthering Heights* to Agatha Christie's eccentric Miss Marple, with her endless knitting and her understated methods of revealing the murder suspects. Each is the central character of her story, and therefore is the heroine. Your heroine can be of the rags-to-riches variety, finding her own methods of revenge on the man who 'done her wrong', as in Barbara Taylor Bradford's *A Woman of Substance*; a victim of circumstance such as the tragedienne in *East Lynne;* or one of the colourful, sexy, uppercrust heroines of Jilly Cooper's novels.

But how do you actually describe your heroine so that the reader readily identifies with her, and doesn't see her as just another blue-eyed blonde or ruthless land-grabber, albeit with a genuine reason for retaining what she sees as rightfully hers?

Straightforward physical description, of course, is easy enough to do. Allowing your heroine to see herself in a mirror or reflection can be overdone, but is frequently used. A more subtle way is to let another character 'see' the heroine and comment or reflect on her appearance, as in the following simple examples.

> `'I can't do a thing with my hair,' Sandy complained. 'I should have had mine cropped really short like yours, Meg, except that I'd end up resembling a boy, and nobody would ever mistake you for anything less than all woman.'`
>
> `'You may be the new owner of the emporium,' the manager told Lavinia coldly, 'but I assure you your father gave me carte blanche to run it the way I pleased, and no little red-haired chit, knee-high to a grasshopper, is going to start dictating to me after all this time.'`

In the first of these two examples something of the physical appearance of the heroine is plainly indicated. Feeding it to the reader in this way is painless and smooth, and doesn't hold up the flow of the story.

In the second example, in one short paragraph, you have an entire situation unfolding, and the reader gets the sense that this girl, however small in statue, is not going to be browbeaten by the manager. His reference to her red hair indicates that he knows she has a mind of her own, and possibly a temper, and by the use of the word 'emporium', there is also the inference that it's probably a Victorian or Edwardian story. A great deal is told about the girl's appearance and character in these few sentences, and you also have the background of the store's management in miniature by the words 'all this time'.

A CHARACTER CHECKLIST

To the beginning author, it's often surprising how few words are needed to conjure up a character in the reader's mind, and this is probably why beginners are often guilty of padding too much. They feel compelled to describe their characters in minute detail, until you feel you could count every strand of her hair. There's no need to put all this down on paper, since it just becomes tedious reading. It may have the effect of filling up the pages, but it does nothing for your story except hold up the action.

But if it's not necessary to put every detail into the final writing, it's vital for you as the author to keep a checklist of everything about your characters alongside you as you write. You may use only a small portion of these points but by writing down as much as you can about your character, and by adding to your list where necessary, she will become ingrained in your own mind, and in turn, this will make her clearer to the reader.

I don't think you do, or should, know everything about your character from the beginning. In real life we get to know people gradually, and in the same way you should be learning about your fictional characters all the time as they develop during the telling of your story. But a good basis of how you want her to shape up is invaluable.

This was my own checklist for my character of Prissy in *Outback Woman*, by Sally Blake, Mills & Boon Masquerade.

> **PRISCILLA BAXTER,** known as Prissy. Nineteen years old. Tired of getting nowhere in her present situation of sweet-voiced singer, play-actress and general dogsbody at a third-rate theatre in London, 1834. Ready for adventure. No family, except the assorted theatricals with whom she lives in lodgings near the theatre in the East End of London.
>
> Curvaceous shape, bright blue eyes. Long dark hair, which she normally wears pinned up except when it becomes unmanageable. Adores her gaudy stage frocks and is adept with her needle due to her practical upbringing with her deceased aunt, who taught her the rudiments of housewifery, and how to read and write.

A bright and breezy Londoner with a quick wit and a soft heart. Not especially looking for romance, but wouldn't knock it if it came looking for her. Has some useful ripe phrases to use on occasion. She's a strong-spirited girl, used to fending for herself, though she often gives the false impression of being over-confident.

She likes a challenge, which she takes up on seeing a poster advertising a five-shilling passage for female emigrants to Australia, Government-paid for those who can't afford the fare, to be deducted from future earnings. (A genuine poster).

She's not afraid to stick up for rights, and to take chances. She's impulsive, which sometimes lands her in hot water. She quite likes children, though hasn't had much to do with them. Her quick way of talking can sometimes irritate people. She's had to put on a tough façade because of the lecherous hangers-on at the theatre, and prides herself on being able to rebuff any man. When she's nervous she's a terrible chatterbox, but in any case, she loves to talk. This too, has sometimes landed her in trouble.

She has a hasty temper. She was what might be called nowadays 'streetwise'. She knew enough about men to know why their eyes darkened at the sight of her in her flimsy stage frocks, and how to keep their unwanted attentions at bay. Physically, she's still a virgin.

This was my first outline of Prissy Baxter, to which I added various other attributes when I was planning the storyline for the book. For instance, I added her birthday, which was useful later on in the story for a minor celebration. I added her enormous sense of humour, which gradually beat down the dour exterior of the Scottish hero in this story. I gave her courage, which she needed to face the outback, both when she was with the hero and when she was alone. I gave her memories, which she could relay to the reader, to flesh out her background and her character and which would make them warm to her. I gave her a romance that was slow to develop, and seemingly highly unlikely to flourish. I gave her a vicarious family to care for, and new friends in an alien country. I gave her a lot of pride.

I don't give every character in my stories such detailed scrutiny, though the central ones in some books need even more of a refined character study. In any case, they all get their share. Even minor ones need to be described and fixed in my own mind so that I know who they are.

It helps me to keep this checklist handy when I'm writing so that I don't begin the book with a heroine with blue eyes and change them to green halfway through. It may sound unlikely, but in practice it's so easy to do, especially in a long book with a large cast of characters.

These more detailed character analyses are quite separate from the straightforward list of characters' names, which is simply that and no more, giving me quick access as to what not to call the next person to appear in the book.

CHAPTER 4

ENTER THE VILLAIN

THE ETERNAL TRIANGLE
THE ANTI-HERO
THE GOTHIC VILLAIN
THE WESTERN VILLAIN
THE LONER
UNSTEREOTYPING THE STEREOTYPES

CHAPTER 4

The essential thing to remember about your characters is that they are going to change in some way before the end of your story. They must grow and develop. Their opinions may well alter drastically during the course of your story as they move through periods of time and circumstances. They must not remain static during these changes. They will form new associations with friends, lovers and enemies, which will all affect them in some way. And into this scenario will inevitably enter the villain.

He doesn't appear in every story, of course. And without conscious thinking I realise I'm labelling him as 'he', though the villain can quite easily be a woman. The wicked stepmother of fairytales is an obvious suggestion, as are the ugly sisters in *Cinderella*.

Without doubt, the villain is an intriguing character to write about. He can sometimes be even more of a three-dimensional character to the author than the hero, and therein lies the first pitfall when planning a triangle story, or a thriller where the villain assumes almost gigantic stature in terms of his very - well, villainy.

You may think that Sherlock Holmes could reasonably have existed without his Watson. But he still needs his Moriarty or similar adversary, if only as the eternal stumbling block against which he performs his superhuman deductions that prove his superiority. The heroic adventurer John Blackthorne, in James Clavell's *Shogun*, would have had far less opportunity to show the readers what he was made of without the evil barbarism of the warlord Toranaga - a brilliant contrast of characters there. And so it goes on.

While it's extremely useful for a hero or heroine to have a confidante - this will be dealt with in the next chapter, an added way for the author to elaborate the hero's strength of character is by allowing him to pit his wits against a ruthless challenger.

Most authors name their villains with rather less attractive names than their heroes. It harks back again to the impression that names make on the reader. A hero called Judas might not command much affection, but transfer his name to the villain, and an association dating back two thousand years is still strong enough to make his name perfectly satisfactory to the reader.

Throwing in a nasty character in a short story or novel just for the sake of it is not enough to make readers interested in him. There has to be a reason for him being there in the first place, so he is as much dependent on the plot as are the other characters in your story.

He is often there in a romantic novel to thwart the hero's attempt to get the girl. In a thriller, he may be undermining the hero's attempts to blow up the important railway line or to hack the computer, or to hijack the aeroplane so that the hero can't get to an important destination in time. He is the one the silent cinema audiences used to hiss at the moment he appeared.

THE ETERNAL TRIANGLE

Most obviously, the villain in an eternal triangle story makes one think of a romantic novel. The villain is the other man, who may or may not have had a past association with the girl. He's the man who will try to win her from the hero at all costs, so he is probably a rake, an evil-doer, a cad, or an out-and-out con man. Any of these types would fit very comfortably into a villain's shoes, whether or not they were two-toned, as beloved by Hollywood movies of the James Cagney ilk; or as completely unshod as a desert sheikh of the early Mills & Boon variety.

In the latter kind of books and movies, most villains wore dark clothes while the heroes wore white robes. Yet in the romantic novels of decades ago, the hero invariably wore a black silk shirt, often open to the waist, or a black polo-necked sweater. In outward appearance, at least, the roles somehow merged, so that it was less easy to spot the villain right away simply by the clothes he wore.

The villain of the piece is never as gilt-edged as the hero. He cannot be, otherwise the logical reader would ask why the heroine didn't fall for him instead of the other one. It's very tempting to make the Other Man or the Other Woman so bad that the character assumes far more interesting proportions than the central two, and this must be avoided at all costs. In a romantic novel, he may be no more than the catalyst to push her towards her true love, or to prevent the story from progressing smoothly, which is the vital ingredient of these novels.

The villain is often the third corner of the detective triangle. Again, the relationship between Sherlock Holmes, Doctor Watson and the dreaded Moriarty is an easy analogy. Throughout the many and varied cases Holmes solved in the Conan Doyle novels, Moriarty's character appears many times. Sometimes he is understated, but he is always an ever-lurking threat to the success of the main protagonists.

An odd phenomenon is the hidden villain. This character is no longer seen, though often fully described, and is as much alive in the reader's imagination as in the author's. The hidden villain's presence distorts the lives of other characters and can put their lives in great danger. A prime example is the way Daphne Du Maurier portrayed the first wife of Maxim de Winter in *Rebecca*. Rebecca is never seen, but her hidden presence is omnipotent throughout the novel, powerful enough almost to destroy the relationship between de Winter and his new wife.

In a different way, the hidden villain appears in E Nesbitt's *The Railway Children*. The true villain of the story is the embezzler who pinned the crime on the children's father and put him in jail. Oddly enough, we hardly 'see' the hero or villain in this novel, yet the actions of this unknown, unseen person affected the lives of an entire family, the triangle in this case being hero, villain, family.

THE ANTI-HERO

The character you also love to hate can be described as the anti-hero. He's a difficult character to create, not all good and not all bad, but one whose appearance can add much to the richness of a story. He is not necessarily a wicked ogre.

In this context, think of Rhett Butler in Margaret Mitchell's *Gone With The Wind*. Part hero, part villain. Despite his appeal to women readers, no one could call him anything but a rogue, and in his character the terms hero and villain definitely overlap. But it also makes him a far more complete character, because even heroes should have their flaws, and sometimes villains can have their saving grace.

Giving two strong male characters interweaving traits in a single story can be tricky. You may lean too far with the wish to show your hero having wicked undertones, and your villain too much compassion. The result is that neither comes through as a distinct leading man. Always keep them firmly placed in your scheme of things when you write your stories, and know in your own mind who is the real hero.

The anti-hero can just as easily be a woman. Fay Weldon certainly had no qualms about that when she invented her infamous She-Devil. Although she was the central character in *The Lives and Loves of a She-Devil*, I don't think many would view her as anything but a villain in heroine's disguise. Yet there was still such a fascination about the She-Devil that the reader was willing her to win through almost as much as we wanted her to get her come-uppance.

THE GOTHIC VILLAIN

The Gothic villain can most simply be described as two-faced, and as such is an interesting character to create. He is often seemingly bland, charming, eager to please, often boyish in appearance ... but underneath all this there lurks an evil heart. His one aim in life is treachery, and he'll stop at nothing to achieve his aims. He has no real saving graces, however pleasant he appears on the surface. The writer of Gothic novels has a huge task in allowing the reader to glimpse little snippets of this evil character's intent, while keeping the denouement and final revelation of his wickedness until the very end of the book.

When the villain appears perfectly charming for much of the book, the reader can be unsure which of two men is the actual wrong 'un. In Gothic novels, the heroine is drawn innocently into the villain's web, and learns the truth about his evil ways only near the end.

This type of story needs to be written with great skill, because although the villain can fool the heroine for almost all of the book, he shouldn't be totally fooling the reader for that long; otherwise the sterling qualities of the hero will be lost. The reader should always be one step ahead of the heroine, even though the circumstances of the plot are leading her into seemingly insurmountable danger.

If you like writing about danger and intrigue, and many twists and turns in a plot, then writing the Gothic novel with its stalwart hero and endangered heroine, and the dastardly villain, may be just for you.

In my Gothic novel *Blackmaddie*, by Rowena Summers, Severn House, (published by Zebra Books, USA; Jean Innes) the villain, Ian, appears at first to be the most elegant, clean-living man anyone could wish to meet at the dour Scottish stronghold of Blackmaddie. This is the first brief description of Ian in his first meeting with the heroine, Charlotte Brodie.

```
Ian was like the sun coming out after rain.
    I did not meet him until dinner that evening, but
immediately I took to this youngest of my three male
cousins, with sandy hair, rather than the bright red of
his brothers, and an innocence of expression in his clear
grey eyes that did not brood like Neil's nor smoulder
like Robert's.
```

Then, towards the end of the book, Charlotte finally sees him for what he is.

```
My breath was rattling in my throat as I gaped at him.
Ian, my cousin Ian, as I had never seen him before. There
was nothing young and innocent about him now. He looked
totally evil, head thrown back and eyes half-closed so
that they glittered in the candlelight, completely naked
beneath a black cloak that was thrown back from his
shoulder. Every part of his body was visible, hair-covered
chest, firm belly ...
```

Between these two revelations of the man, there are many dark hints along the way as to just who the villain is; but it is not until near the end that it all becomes clear. It's not easy to include these pointers for the reader's benefit, but it's essential. You cannot mislead the reader indefinitely.

She must be able to think back over the events in the book, and realise that the clues were there all the time, if only she had realised it. It's down to the skill of the author to make sure she's never *quite* sure until the end of the book. Convincing characterisation of the Gothic villain, is sometimes the hardest thing to achieve, because of this dual role he has to play.

And if there was ever a case for getting into the skin of your characters, I think this is it. In villainous terms, you may find this extremely difficult to do, but it's the only way for you to understand how your character would behave at any time in your story. How he deceives, charms, and eventually, reveals all (with no pun intended from the above passage in *Blackmaddie*).

THE WESTERN VILLAIN

This is the character essential to all stories about cowboys and Indians. Without the baddie there would be no gun fights at the ol' corral, no squabbles over land and water rights, no Indian braves carrying off maidens in the night. There would be none of the lawlessness on which the premise of the Wild West, in fiction at least, has always thrived.

Since the Western story is always American, it's vital to get the language right when you depict your characters. Whether he is a gun-man, a cattle-thief, a bounty hunter, an outlaw, a ruthless mercenary, a gambler with a mean streak, or a train - or stage-coach robber, he is not going to mince words or give his adversary much time for thinking. Western villains live with danger. They ride hard, shoot first, and ask questions later.

This is no time for the timid author to try to put too many saving graces into a character. The villains in Western stories have few traits to make them worthy characters. Those that they do have may be a sense of filial loyalty, as in the case of the legendary James brothers. Or the villain who has turned from being the good guy to one carrying out a vendetta because of some injustice done to him or his family in the past. The villain with a mission of revenge comes high on the Western writer's agenda.

They call their fathers Pa, their mothers are generally Ma. They may be called Chuck or Red or any number of nicknames, which were very common in Western culture. Sometimes they were simply called by their surnames, often beginning with the harder-sounding consonants, such as Grant, Carver, Kincade, Quincy. Names also included those pertaining to their birth state. Characters in Western fiction often have such appendages as Colorado or Tex or Arizona, which immediately help to identify them to the reader.

The Western villain may have a longstanding grudge or a score to settle, or he may simply be the type of man who enjoys killing for killing's sake. And in the days of remote communities that sprang up almost overnight by the discovery of gold, or fertile farming land in a parched desert area, it's easy to see how desperate men could try to get the upper hand by sheer force. This is the stuff of Western villains, against whom our stalwart hero eventually wins through.

If you write Western stories, be prepared to use some pretty strong dialogue between your characters. Don't be tempted to pretty it up for the sake of propriety. Realism demands some ripe expletives, which can be quite inventive on the part of the author, but still kept in the seemingly authentic Western mode. Incidentally, much of Georgette Heyer's hugely accepted Regency slang was copied by later authors as authentic, but was often her own invention. The Western author too, can invent 'authentic' idioms and phrases that are colourful and visual. They may not be your particular style, but they take the place of vast explanations, and bring a character and scene vividly to life.

```
• Necktie parties (hangings).
• As horny a critter as a spiny anteater.
• He handled his gun with all the finesse he'd handle a
  saloon woman, and that ain't much.
• As low as a snake's belly and twice as 'ornery.
• He had a penchant for Kansas sheep dip (cheap
  whisky).
```

Western villains may move in groups or as loners. The groups may be the vigilantes who took the law into their own hands when they felt real justice wasn't being meted out soon enough and whose efforts often ended up in the 'necktie parties' referred to above. The vigilante ideal was intended to be for good, but frequently turned bad, especially when an unscrupulous leader used the group for his own ends. But some authorities still welcomed the vigilante groups, finding it easier to sit back and let the gang do their dirty work for them.

The vigilante groups were often on the fringe of true villainy, since their aims could be rough, swift justice as an alternative to the laborious processes of the law. One of their less savoury habits was the public display of photographs of their dead victims as a dire warning to others not to cross them, and also to show their strength.

The more responsible of the groups may truly have wanted to bring wrongdoers to justice, but in fiction, it's the wrong 'uns who are the most satisfying to write about. The lone hero faced with such a lawless mob has an entire gang to pit his wits against.

THE LONER

The lone villain, whether in a Western story or in any other, can have all the evil traits you want to give him. He can be the man who stalks his prey for months or years until he finally shoots him dead. He can terrorise whole communities, perpetrating every kind of terrible crime along the way, until he finally gets his man. Or more probably, he doesn't - because in a story of this kind, you would almost certainly have the hero stalking the villain just as cleverly, and it would be the hero who eventually won in the final showdown.

The loner can be all bad, or he can have a sense of tragedy about him. What has turned him bad? And what has kept him that way? Does his ego swell with every new killing? Is he becoming weary of always being on the run, always needing to be one step ahead of the sheriff/Interpol/ private eye/amateur female sleuth?

Is he a psychopathic killer, crazed with his own power behind a gun? Is he entirely merciless, relishing the slow killing of his victim, or does he have any compassion at all? Does he enjoy terrorising women and dragging them off trains, stage-coaches or cars stranded on motorways, or out of their remote farmhouses?

For all his wickedness, the villain undoubtedly has courage, nerve, cunning and strength, even though he may be a drifter, a gambler, a hired gunman or a petty thief. He knows what his fate will be if the law ever catches up with him, and is aware that he'll die, whether by the gun, the rope, or after life imprisonment. He knows he's doomed. Unless, of course, he's the other kind of loner ...

This is the landowner who grows fat and prosperous while he pays those around him to do his foul deeds, and thinks he can get away with anything because of his seeming respectability. He's as ruthless as the man who actually pulls the gun on his enemies, but he appears to be an upright citizen, smoking his huge cigars and posturing about in fine clothes. He can be blatantly obvious to the reader as the bad guy, or he can be a little like the Gothic villain, in that we're never quite sure of his true nature until the end of the story.

The many types of villain give you ample scope for imaginative writing, and for inventing devious storylines incorporating the worst characteristics you can devise. It's a further continuation of those cops-and-robbers or cowboys-and-Indian pictures we used to see on Saturday mornings, and acting out some of their own childhood fantasies can give the authors of such stories enormous pleasure.

Always take your characters seriously, but at the same time, enjoy your writing. Creating any characters of the villainous kind can also be enormous fun to write about because they're inevitably larger than life, flamboyant and infinitely interesting, with all the varying facets of human nature coursing through their evil veins and their black hearts.

UNSTEREOTYPING THE STEREOTYPES

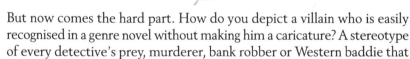

But now comes the hard part. How do you depict a villain who is easily recognised in a genre novel without making him a caricature? A stereotype of every detective's prey, murderer, bank robber or Western baddie that has gone before?

The simple answer is that there is no simple answer. One way is to give him a background that's unique and unusual, and which will colour his future actions, making him more believable to the reader. A relationship that went sour perhaps; a wife killed accidentally, the tragic events turning his mind so that he continually pursues the imagined murderer.

Except in the case of Gothic novels, and in the fast-moving, twist-in-the-tale short stories that are normally printed on a single magazine page, most villains are quickly recognisable within the first few pages of a novel. And even in some of the short-short magazine stories, the reader is often left in no doubt who the villain is, and the only surprise is just how and when he's going to do his dastardly deed.

Making a villain physically ugly isn't necessary. He can be as ordinary as the man sitting next to you on the bus. It's what's in his heart that's evil, so don't feel you have to scar his cheek or give him a lopsided limp or a patch over one eye, unless that sort of physical disfigurement happens to be part of his character and essential to your story.

You can give him a voice that's unique to him, and perhaps different from the one the reader is expecting. Create a Western villain with a soft southern drawl or a cultured European accent, perhaps, instead of the guttural tones the reader would be expecting. You can dress him in a different garb from the expected. You can devise different ways of letting him perform his villainous tasks.

A murderer with a neat line in incision, perhaps, that might come only from a surgeon's skill with a scalpel - or a master butcher ... ; a spy with a personalised and obviously nasty method of dealing with people who get in his way; poisons that are undetectable, whether swift or slow - all of these are predictable, and it would be up to you to think up new ways of administering them that would give an extra twist to the villain's expertise. I offer only suggestions, not solutions.

A villain's dealings with other people may be different from the expected. He may be courteous or foppish by day; ruthless by night or when he has his darker tasks to perform. A character who demonstrates this duel role perfectly, is the hero of *The Scarlet Pimpernel*.

The Mexican bandit is readily recognised by his drooping moustache and unshaven appearance. Such stereotypes are hard to disguise, as are most ethnic ones. Race and colour will obviously influence your decision on your characters if you are writing a story about mixed cultures. But it's as unrealistic to have every villain coloured black as to think that every Caucasian is pure white, in character as well as appearance.

Thankfully, the days when you needed to portray your villain as being black of hair and skin are gone. Your fictional housemaid may just as easily be a college student wanting to earn some pin money during the college vacation - and just as capable of an unplanned murder if she's in the right place, in the right circumstances, and at the right time. To make your villain convincing to you and your readers, the villain is deserving of a detailed checklist, just as much as your main characters. Get to know him and all his evil ways. If he begins to make you shudder, then you're on your way to making your readers shudder too.

This was my initial checklist for the heinous character of Ian Stewart in *Blackmaddie*.

IAN STEWART. Youngest of the three brothers living at the Scottish castle of Blackmaddie. Handsome, red-haired like all the Stewart men. Charming, anxious to please. Outwardly friendly to all. So amusing that at times he seems almost childlike despite being a powerfully built young man. Seemingly the least complex of them all at Blackmaddie, but his demeanour hides the blackest heart, to be revealed near the end of the book. Heavily in witchcraft. Father of the servant girl's child, unknown to anyone else in the family. Obsessed with evil-doing. Slowly and methodically undermining the heroine's feeling of sanity, and determined to kill her. Canny enough to know it mustn't happen too soon, thus arousing suspicion. As the book builds to a climax and his various attempts to frighten/kill Charlotte are foiled, he will be revealed as the Master, the Evil One.

CHAPTER 5

THE REST OF THE CAST

HOW FEW? HOW MANY?
THE CONFIDANTE CHARACTER
THE MINOR CHARACTERS
THE WALK-ONS

CHAPTER 5

HOW FEW? HOW MANY?

As well as thinking in scenes for whatever kind of fiction I'm writing, which tends to keep the writing tight and controlled, I think of all my characters in theatrical terms. I have my main characters, my minor ones, and my walk-ons. For me, this terminology very definitely keeps them in all their correct places.

The main characters, are, of course, those who will have the greatest importance in any story. They are the ones on which all the actions will focus. They are the stars. The kings and queens of fiction, with all the rest of their subjects in descending order of priority as far as importance is concerned.

But characters don't, and shouldn't, live in a vacuum. They have families, friends, acquaintances, business associates, enemies, and an entire personal history before your story begins. They also have an entire future to live out after your story has ended, which means you should never leave them high and dry, with nothing really resolved at the end of it all.

Because of all this necessary interaction between the characters in a story, it's often a puzzle to new writers to know just how many of these subsidiary characters to include, and even more, just how much importance should be given to them.

As a very simple guideline, the shorter the piece of fiction the fewer characters that are needed. It's a great mistake to clutter up a short story for a magazine with a whole host of characters who have little or nothing to do with the main action, simply because the author thinks they would bring interesting colour to it. They won't. They'll just make the story over-busy and irritating to read. They'll detract from the importance of the main protagonists, and they'll diffuse the main issue.

A tightly controlled short story involving no more than two characters, with a real story to tell, can be a masterpiece. A meandering short story involving a cast of thousands will be a total disaster.

I'm not advocating, however, that you keep strictly to two characters in a magazine story. Very often a story can be improved greatly by the addition of several more characters, and it's impossible to generalise without knowing the storyline the author intends to write. But that old saying that you can't see the wood for the trees is as true when it comes to cluttering up a short story with too many characters as it is for any other analogy.

The number of characters you use in a novel depends solely on the novel. How long is a piece of string ... ? A short romantic novel of 55,000 words demands far fewer characters than a family saga of more than three times that number, when all the twists and turns of competing family members for an inheritance, for instance, hinges on many individual character traits and circumstances.

A spy thriller can take up as many characters as the action dictates. A time travel novel can involve an entire world of people, robots, mutants, or whatever your imagination devises, both in the narrow confines of a spaceship or space station, and later, in a new and alien environment.

Since market study is essential in targeting your short stories at the right source, it's an interesting exercise to go through the published stories in a pile of magazines, counting the number of characters each author has used. This can be also done with novels, though it would probably become tedious and spoil your enjoyment of the story.

Jilly Cooper does all this for you in her novel *Rivals*, where she lists all the characters and their relationships as a frontispiece to the book. It's not usual to list all the characters in a novel in this way, but it's interesting to try to see the characters through the names and lifestyles the author uses. It is also interesting to see the complete cast-list at a glance. The average reader, absorbed in a novel without bothering about any of the techniques involved, would probably be startled at the number and variety of characters an author invents in order to create a whole world between the covers of a book.

The type of characters created in radio stories are obviously meant to appeal to the ear and not the eye. This is a different medium from written fiction, and if it is the kind you want to write for, I suggest you read a specialised book on the subject. All that is necessary to say here is that the characters have to come to life for the listeners by the strength of their voices alone. This also serves to underline all that was said about the power of the voice in an earlier chapter.

But the general rule about numbers remains the same. The shorter the play, the fewer characters should be used, in order to portray each one as vividly as possible for the listener.

THE CONFIDANTE CHARACTER

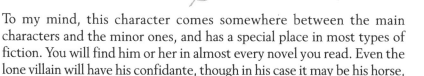

To my mind, this character comes somewhere between the main characters and the minor ones, and has a special place in most types of fiction. You will find him or her in almost every novel you read. Even the lone villain will have his confidante, though in his case it may be his horse, or his gun, or the wild prairie. Whoever hears all the main character's innermost thoughts and secrets is the confidante character.

You may remember a song in the film *Paint Your Wagon* called 'I Talk To The Trees', sung by Clint Eastwood. I don't think that was written tongue-in-cheek, without a shrewd insight into the way the character was thinking at the time. There was no one else in whom he could confide right then, so he rode off by himself - and talked to the trees. This is hardly an unheard of phenomenon, even in more exalted circles, and is not at all as crazy as it sounds, since it had the effect of bringing the character's innermost thoughts out into the open, and allowing him to see two sides of his problem.

How many times in real life do we find ourselves talking to ourselves and answering our own problems? We become, at such times, our own confidante character.

The detective and his sometimes long-suffering sidekick have been mentioned before. There are many other duos in whom one of the two acts as the confidante character. The New York cop and his partner; the small girl and her imaginary playmate; the secretary and her flatmate; the schoolboy and his inseparable best friend; the hospital patient and the understanding nurse.

The listeners in all such fictional partnerships share the same role. They allow the main character to explain things to the reader in a way that gains the reader's sympathy and understanding. The confidante may not always be in a position to respond, as in the case of the villain 'talking it out' to his horse; or the small girl with the imaginary playmate.

But, while the main character is telling things to this confidante, using sometimes emotional dialogue and telling secrets he wouldn't tell to anyone else, he is revealing more of his character to the reader in the process.

Sometimes the confidante is there merely as a sounding board, and he will be in a far lesser role at that time. But sometimes the things he hears and the way he responds can reveal a great deal about both speaker and listener.

In my book *The Bannister Girls*, (WH Allen/Grafton), are three well-to-do sisters, Angel, Ellen and Louise. The year is 1915, which dictates the innocence of the characters. In the illustrative scene below, the young and beautiful Angel Bannister is surprised by her normally feisty sister's question on how it feels to make love. Ellen is the confidante character, but there's a great deal of blurring at the edges as to whose character is becoming clearer to the reader - deliberately so in this case, because this is a family saga where the sisters have roles of almost equal importance.

Ellen looked thoughtful, a grass blade held tightly between her teeth. She lay back on the grass, wanting to know something, having to ask the question that had been burning inside her ever since Angel's indiscretion had been discovered, the subject becoming a taboo one within the family. Now seemed as good a time as any.

'Angel, what's it like to lie with a man? You don't have to tell me if you don't want to, but I'm dying with curiosity, and it was never something I could ask Rose. Not before Ronnie died, and certainly not after. Louise would never discuss such things, even if I cared to bring up the subject. Besides, I can't imagine that Stanley's the most scintillating lover. I know you know all about it, and I really wish you'd tell me.'

Her voice stopped abruptly, and Angel's first feeling of acute embarrassment gave way to surprise as she caught the uncertainty in Ellen's voice. Why, her sister really was curious, and a little afraid. It was the way Angel herself had been before she was thrust into the situation with Jacques, almost before she had time to think.

Until now, she hadn't even considered that she had knowledge of which her superior and clever sister was totally ignorant, and the flippant retort to Ellen to mind her own business died on her lips. They lay side by side, not looking at one another, and Angel's voice was soft and dreamy.

> 'It's like being on the edge of a precipice and finding
> that the fall is a delight and not terrifying after all.
> It's like floating somewhere in space. It's like touching
> the stars. It's exciting, and humbling, and being a part
> of someone else, and wanting him so badly that you ache
> for him every minute of the day. And it's a feeling that
> can only happen when two people are right for one another.
> When you're so much in love that the thought of sin never
> enters your head.'

You may think that Angel was the confidante character, simply because she was being asked the question. But she's not. She's informing the reader of her innermost feelings in a way she would never normally do. She's revealing that she's a true romantic, whom the reader instinctively knows is going to remain true to her lover, despite the fact that he's doing a dangerous job in a war and she may never see him again ...

In a historical novel, the confidante character is often an elderly relative in whom the younger person can confide; or a maid, who is seemingly as insignificant as the wallpaper, or who alternatively speaks up and gives her pert opinion. Whatever role you define for the confidante character, be assured that he or she plays an important part in your story. She tells the reader things about the main characters that they wouldn't necessary want revealed to each other at that time, or perhaps their own inhibitions simply prevent them from speaking up.

You may be asking yourself, how an extra confidante character can appear in a short story where there are no two characters anyway? Physically, he can't. But imagine that the main character is a girl who's just received a threatening blackmail letter, the details of which involve a past relationship. She daren't tell the new man in her life, who is the other main character, and there's no one else to confide in. There are various ways to overcome this.

Your character can go through the thought processes of the past relationship and all that the future will entail because of the blackmail threat. This idea doesn't involve a physical confidante and is perfectly adequate, but if it's too prolonged, it will involve too much narrative and hold up the forward action.

She can pick up a photograph of herself and her old love together, and 'speak' to him. She can find his old letters and read them, and you can write bits of the letters in your story as if they are actual dialogue interspersed with her thoughts. She can remember places where they went, evoking scents and sounds, again with mini-scenes of dialogue.

She can put on a special record, and remember snatches of conversation, which you will write into the story. She can see something on television that reminds her of him, again bringing in remembered dialogue. She can talk aloud to photos, diaries, letters, as if he's actually there, revealing her emotions at the time, regrets, fear, despair, panic.

All of this will tell the reader something of what's happening *now*, what happened *then*, and her fears for the future. Any of these choices use an unseen confidante character that nevertheless will become very real to the reader. Use them sparingly, emotionally, and obviously not all at once.

THE MINOR CHARACTERS

These are the people who surround and support your main characters. The minor characters of greatest importance will usually be named, and form an important part of any story. Some may not be named, but are still essential for furthering a specific part of the plot.

Minor characters may be family members, office colleagues, the rest of the football team, the people the main characters meet in a confined setting, such as a cruise ship or aeroplane. They can be present throughout the length of the story, but not always. Even though they may play a vital part in pushing along the action in a story - or delaying it - they may logically then disappear.

Sometimes they take on a brief and useful role, producing an unwilling revelation from the main character, almost pushing her into revealing something of herself against her will. They are not as understanding as the true confidante. Rather, they goad the main character into some discussion.

In my book *All In The April Morning* (WH Allen/Star), the heroine, Bridget and her small, sleeping sister are being driven to their new home in New York State by a friend of a friend. They have only just met this brash young man, but he's a useful minor character and drags out Bridget's worst memories by his insistent questions. The year is 1907.

Although the light was fading, she tried to take some interest in the vineyards and peach orchards. Roadside stalls were shut up for the night, on which presumably grapes and peaches would be offered for sale in the morning. Bridget's mouth watered. It seemed a very long way from Mrs Dowdy's mediocre cooking, or the soup kitchens provided by generous San Franciscans for the homeless immigrants.

Marcus realised she was becoming more silent as the journey went on. He was burning with curiosity, wondering if he dared ask this strange, beautiful girl what he wanted to know. Finally he thought, what the hell? Ask or stay dumb!

'Say, what was it like - being in an earthquake? We read about it in the papers, but I've never met anybody who actually experienced it. Was it truly horrific?'

Her lips felt as if they were made of lumps of ice. Yet inside, she was burning with rage. It was ghoulish of him to ask, when she'd just told him she'd lost her parents in the earthquake. She met his eyes in the mirror, and guessed he was no more curious than most people, and the words tumbled out.

'Terrifying's more like it - I never want to live through anything like it again.' She chewed her lip. She hadn't wanted to die either, and that had been the alternative.

'But how did it *feel*? Were houses really thrown up in the air before they collapsed like doll houses?'

His face came back into focus. 'Yes, they were, houses and cars and people,' she said harshly. 'It tore everything to bits, including my mammie and daddy, and small brother. Now, is there anything else you want to know?'

'Hey kid, I'm sorry. I didn't think. They said San Francisco was a beautiful city before ... '

Sweet Jesus didn't he know when to leave it alone! Bridget hardly ever blasphemed, but the words slid angrily through her mind at that moment.

'Perhaps it was. I only know I never want to see it again. I'll never go back.'

Marcus glanced at the taut figure in the back of the prized open-top. With all that pain in her darkened eyes, Bridget O'Connell wasn't just a pretty kid, she was beautiful. But he wished to God he'd never brought up the subject of the earthquake.

'You won't ever have to,' he reminded her. 'You'll be taken care of now.'

Bridget looked down at Kitty, sleeping exhaustedly in her arms.

'That's what happens to poor people, isn't it?' She said slowly, not really accepting until that moment that they were poor.

This scene tells a great deal about Bridget O'Connell's present feelings, and the long-lasting effects of experiencing the great San Francisco earthquake of 1906. Her feelings are emphasised by the insensitive minor character, Marcus, urging her on. After the car journey, he will be no longer important to this story, and will never appear in it again, but here he makes an important contribution.

Always make sure that your minor characters never take over from your main ones. This is a danger when you suddenly find you have a special interest in a minor one who seems so much more interesting than you thought at first that you decide to give him a larger part to play in the story.

Suddenly you have two heroes, vying against each other for prominence in your story. Sometimes neither wins, and you're left bewildered, wondering why your hero is no longer as clear-cut as he was when you first thought of him. Your minor character has edged through, and he must be cut down and kept in his place.

If this sounds as if the characters have assumed lives of their own, taken off into doing their own thing, then believe me, it happens. Indeed, it *must* happen if you are to make your fictional characters believable to someone else. Until now, they have existed only in your own imagination, but once they become so real to you that they live and breathe in your head, you're on the right road to making them live for your readers.

THE WALK-ONS

It can be a great temptation to insert into your story fascinating little details of every person you bring into it, and to include totally unnecessary characters in the mistaken idea that they make the story more interesting. For instance, let's say that in the interests of realism a new writer may decide to include in her story a man who has just come to live in the empty house next door to the main character. The main character is a senior executive in an electronics firm in which sabotage is suspected. It's his story, and the man next door will play no part in it. He's not a detective in disguise or a long-lost son or father; he's just an extra - not even a walk-on in this case. He's a nuisance factor to the forward flow of the story.

But the new writer decides that a man next door might be an interesting diversion to write about. This new character, whose only role is that of a new neighbour, is then described by the new writer as Hodson, or Hatson, or maybe Hobday, or something like that. (The NW is putting in all these alternatives to illustrate that he's not all that important a character). Anyway, she goes on as follows ...

```
   Hodson, or Hatson or Hobday, has an interesting crook to
his nose, and he's stooping so badly, you wonder why he
doesn't use a walking stick or get his spine straightened
out. They have surgeons these days who can work wonders.
The woman at the corner shop - they open on Sundays now,
by the way - had her bunions done and was practically
running around the next day. Anyway, this man, Hodson,
or Hatson, or whatever, used to run a market garden -
it was in Cornwall, or it might have been Devon, had a
heart attack after his wife left him, and it was a near
thing too.
   He found a new girlfriend who ran off with his money,
and almost committed suicide. Luckily he was found by his
cleaning lady, a Mrs Morris, no relation to the riverside
Morrises as far as is known - who, incidentally, won five
hundred pounds at bingo the other week, and is going
to Majorca for a week in the summer, though she'll be
totally out of place, having never gone farther than
Blackpool ...
```

Are you exhausted and bored by all this? You should be. Perhaps you think I have gone too far in making a point. But this is the kind of cluttering trivia that is unfortunately seen all too often in the manuscripts of new writers. They think it essential to detail all these superfluous characters and their dreary doings. They are not of the remotest interest to the reader, and all this side-tracking is merely delaying what is of most interest, namely the drama going on at the electronics firm, and its effect on the main character. By now the reader would have forgotten all about the real purpose of the story.

If the man arriving next door has a vital part to play, we may need to know that he's there - but we don't need to know his entire life history, and certainly not that of a cleaning woman! What has she got to do with anything when the story is about to hinge around a far more elaborate sabotage plot?

Of course, this is a very exaggerated and contrived example of bringing in extraneous characters for the sake of it - in other words, padding the pages to make it seem like an interesting story when, in fact, the padding has exactly the opposite effect. You could probably make three or four separate stories out of the clutter in that one example. But I don't mean to be unjust or unkind to new writers, because they're certainly not the only guilty ones ...

Walk-ons are rarely named in stories. They are people who certainly need to be included, but who can safely remain as shadowy participants as opposed to the sharply defined main characters, and the slightly lesser outlines of the others.

Walk-ons are the landlords at the inn, the maid who turns down the bedclothes in the hotel, the receptionist at the dentist, the ship's purser, the raw recruit, the constable at the desk of the police station, and any other subsidiary character who may need to be mentioned in passing, but who is relatively unimportant to the main flow of the story.

Yes, if your story warrants it, these people have their parts to play. You can't let your stage-coach be driven at breakneck speed with a horde of Indians screaming for your hero's blood without a driver desperately holding on to the horses' reins. But unless he's personally known to the hero, or if he himself is the hero, or fulfils the role of a minor character, then he's just the driver. The reader doesn't need to know his name. We certainly don't need to be told he's had a thumping toothache for two days, and that after this run, he's heading for town to get it fixed in good time for the weekly hoe-down. The driver of the stage-coach would be a genuine walk-on, because the coach couldn't get to its destination without him. But be very careful about how many of these people you include, and about making them into nuisance factors as in the example given earlier. Be especially careful with the little 'asides' that creep into the telling of the story, in which so-called fascinating snippets on character and background are included. If they concern the important characters, and mean something to the plot, that's fine. If they don't, be ruthless and get rid of them.

It's a useful exercise to read published works and see how experienced writers deal with these different types of characters. In particular, notice the walk-ons and how easily they can be dealt with. They are important only as extras, often without speaking parts; but then fill in the gaps so that we don't have riderless horses, or meals miraculously served without waiters, or a battlefield with a heroic captain performing superhuman deeds of courage without a platoon to back him up. What a waste, if no one were there to observe it, anyway!

We often need these walk-on characters later in the book. A maid can be called as a witness to a hotel robbery or murder. Members of the army platoon can confirm that their captain didn't desert, but was captured by enemy soldiers - more walk-ons - until he staggered back through the jungle, half crazed ...

If you open your mind and let your imagination roam, you can create any number of situations where a shadowy walk-on character is needed, but he can logically be made to disappear without affecting the plot or diffusing the main characters in any way. He has his place, despite his apparent insignificance. But then, no character in *your* story is going to be insignificant, is he?

CHAPTER 6

POINTS OF VIEW

FIRST PERSON, THIRD PERSON
THE SINGLE-VIEWPOINT ROLE
THE MULTI-VIEWPOINT NARRATIVE
CHOOSING THE VIEWPOINT CHARACTER

CHAPTER 6

FIRST PERSON, THIRD PERSON

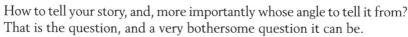

How to tell your story, and, more importantly whose angle to tell it from? That is the question, and a very bothersome question it can be.

Some years ago, when I was writing stories for the so-called 'confession', or 'true-life' magazines, the answer was obvious. All these stories were supposed to be written from the narrator's viewpoint, as she - or he - poured out her heart to a friend - the reader.

In my opinion that was the true juxtaposition of writer and reader in these stories - the writer/narrator became the confessor, and the reader became the best friend. In other words, the reader also became the confidante, taking over in real life one of the roles we create in our fictional characters.

Because of this specialised form of writing, confession stories were always written in the first person - the I character. They couldn't be written in any other way. It's a great way to become the character you're writing about and to think of her as yourself, which you must necessarily do. It's easier to get inside her skin, wearing her shoes, going about her everyday business, meeting her friends.

In donning the I role, you can become wife, lover, business partner, accomplice, murderer, or whatever fits the character in your story. The reader identifies readily with the narrator in a first-person story. If the writer is swept along by the power and passion of her narration, the reader is also drawn into that creative world that belongs to them both for the duration of the story.

True-life stories did not always involve the characters in sexual affairs in the old implied 'sin, suffer and repent' idea. They involved many areas of social problems through which the central character had to live, come to terms with problems, and eventually solve them. To this end, there was a great deal of emotional content in these stories, which I will deal with in a later chapter. Suffice it now to say that one of the main difficulties of the writer using the first-person style of writing is the need to forget your own personality, and immerse yourself in that of the character you in effect become.

The first-person narrative is not only confined to the true-life kind of story. I have used it many times in more general short stories, and it is a personal choice whether or not you feel comfortable with it. It's also sensible to study the magazines you are writing for to make sure they accept first-person stories, as not all editors like them.

It's important to remember the use of tenses when using first-person narrative. The purists will say that a narrator couldn't be recording a tense scene of drama as it happened, for instance, and thus expressing it in the present tense. Yet some quite emotional published stories have been successfully written in this way, but unless it is done very skilfully, they can give the reader an uncomfortable feeling of stretching belief.

More usually, a story that begins vividly in the present tense would then go into flashback and the more conventional past tense before being brought full circle in the denouement.

The Writers' and Artists' Yearbook and *The Writer's Handbook* give you broad details as to whether magazines require first-or-third-person narratives in their short stories, as do the guidelines issued by some of these magazines. You can write to request these guidelines, if available, from the magazine of your choice; the address will be given somewhere inside it. It's preferable to direct your letter to the fiction editor, who is usually named, remembering to include a fairly large stamped addressed envelope for a reply.

As well as short stories, I have also written novels from the first-person viewpoint. I took the role of a young boy in my teenage novel *The Fugitives* (by Jean Saunders, William Heinemann). I was a young man in my historical novel, *Sands of Lamanna* (by Jean Innes, Robert Hale), and a young woman in *White Blooms of Yarrow* (by Jean Innes, Robert Hale). I became Charlotte Brodie in *Blackmaddie*, since most, but not all, Gothic novels are written in the first person.

So what are the advantages and disadvantages of writing in the first person? Firstly, because of the great intimacy involved in 'becoming' another person in the shape of your character, there's the need to rid yourself of any inhibitions.

If your main character is a vicious thug, you must mentally put yourself into his shoes and imagine how he would feel mugging an old lady for pennies. If he is a spy, you must sense the adrenaline flowing, the fear, the danger, the excitement and thrill of the treasonable offences he undertakes. If she is a passionate young woman in the throes of a love affair, you must be prepared to write scenes that may not even be within your own experience, and not to skim over them because of the worry that great-aunt Ethel might be offended.

Of course, this kind of realism comes into every kind of writing, but it's very much more personalised when it's written in the first person, and can result in certain quizzical reactions from friends and family. When jovial acquaintances look at me sideways after reading one of my more earthy novels, and ask me where I get my experience from, I look them straight in the eye and tell them Agatha Christie didn't need to commit murder in order to write about it.

The nitty-gritty about first-person narrative is that everything your main character sees, hears, smells, touches, senses, and so on can come only through her own experience. In some ways this limits your writing, but it can also be a challenge to think up ways in which she can play an essential part in the plot. And she *must* do so, since it's her story.

The narrator can obviously overhear things. She can see newspaper reports. She can have discussions with other people in order to learn things. She can be mobile, moving in different settings, depending on the plot. She can have thought sequences - even dream sequences in moderation. Never be tempted to overdo dream sequences, and never begin your story with your character living through a dream sequence, because the reader will feel cheated when she realises this isn't yet the 'real' story.

One of the biggest problems with the first person viewpoint is simply the overuse of the word I. If you use it to begin every paragraph it can become very cumbersome and the readers will soon get bored with it. If only for this reason, try to vary the way you begin paragraphs. Since I am writing this book, I am obviously the first-person narrator, but it hasn't been necessary, and certainly not desirable, to begin every paragraph with I. In fact, in this chapter so far, I haven't begun a single paragraph that way.

Since it is obviously vital to know the name of your main character in any story, this hurdle must be overcome in some way. It's very old-fashioned to state boldly: 'I, Jean Saunders ... ' unless, of course, you were starting a story with your character reading out a statement in court, when this would be perfectly feasible.

Otherwise, you really need to have another character in dialogue with your I person, to let the reader in on who he or she is. Or she could be reading a newspaper story aloud that named her, or whatever other way you devise. Until that moment, even the gender of the main character may be in doubt, so don't leave it too long before you make it quite clear who your main character is.

But how do you let your readers know what your I character looks like without resorting to her seeing her reflection in a mirror - the most obvious, and most over-used method (but still perfectly acceptable if done with skill)? You would do it by the comments of other characters; or by letting her study photographs of herself and bemoaning her flaws; or by the narrator stating flatly that her doting father has a rose-coloured view of her. Such as -

> I didn't have a small nose at all, and it did turn up annoyingly at the tip. And my eyes weren't that sickeningly cornflower blue, but a sort of dark, smoky, grey ...

In this way you would be telling the reader something about the two characters, while revealing the appearance of the heroine.

As for the old mirror trick - your first-person heroine doesn't always have to see herself as beautiful, ravishing and desirable. Sometimes it's good to give your readers the shock treatment, and endear the character to them in the process. The following example would fit smoothly into a historical novel.

> I rushed upstairs and leaned against my bedroom door to catch my breath, and immediately saw myself in the long mirror. What an impression to make on a prospective beau! I'd ridden hard over the moors, and my hair was a wild tangle of unkempt curls. There was an unladylike film of perspiration on my skin, which was unnaturally flushed from its usual delicate pallor. A large smudge of dirt on my chin did nothing for my angular features. I thought furiously, even though it did have the effect of shortening my face. Some might say the result was attractive, even pixie-like. I allowed myself a touch of grudging generosity before I lost all my self-confidence.

The reader would learn a great deal from that brief piece of description, which takes nothing away from the first-person narrative. The girl is acting as the observer here, letting the reader see her exactly in the poor light she sees herself.

When it comes to writing in the third person, things become a little easier. Although the writer necessarily distances himself a little from the narrator in this case, there's also a feeling of safety in naming your characters with your chosen tags, and writing about them as if they are people you know, rather than yourself. Although you should still know and understand your characters, third-person narrative is a less personal form of writing. You don't have quite the same embarrassing feeling of putting yourself into a love scene, or sailing the high seas as a pirate, or stealing something from the local supermarket, or busking, because the character is named as someone else, not I.

In many ways, the first-person narrative gives you a narrower focus, while the third-person gives you more freedom. General short stories can be written from either viewpoint.

Novels, except for Gothics, are more usually written from the third-person viewpoint, simply because of the greater freedom that it affords. There's certainly a feeling of immediacy and involvement about the first-person narrative, and in the end it's a personal choice for the author.

Many successful novels have been written in the first-person narrative, such as Wendy Perriam's *After Purple*, and Susan Howatch's *The Rich Are Different*. Novels that we now regard as classics were written with first-person narrative - *Jane Eyre*, *Cranford*, *Kidnapped*, etc.

As a final pointer as to which choice may be right for you, remember that you can sometimes slip too many of your own opinions into the first-person narrative, with the result that it becomes arrogant or egotistical. With third-person, you can still stand back a little from your characters and play God, directing them much as a stage director directs his cast in a play. It's up to you to find the most convincing way to write your own story and develop your own writing style.

One last important note for budding romantic novelists. Mills & Boon romantic novels, and their Masquerade historicals, are always written from the third-person viewpoint. There are no exceptions to this rule.

THE SINGLE-VIEWPOINT ROLE

Following on from the last statement is the tricky question of unwittingly switching viewpoints. It's very easy, when writing a story, to slip from the central character's viewpoint into someone else's, bringing in his thoughts, opinions and aspirations. A short story, which may cover no more than a single dramatic incident or conflict between two people, should only ever use the main character's viewpoint. You should always be very clear in your mind who is the central character, and therefore, who is taking control of the actions in the story.

Most short novels, and certainly Mills and Boon novels, use the single-viewpoint technique. This undoubtedly simplifies the action, and doesn't send the reader off into other realms of consciousness, as in the example of the extraneous nuisance characters in the last chapter. But I will just qualify that statement, because more recently there has been a movement in Mills & Boon stories for the hero to have more of a viewpoint role than that which they once had. The heroine is still, and, unless policy changes, will always be the central character; but, as in any real-life romance, it is desirable for both sides of a partnership to be shown to have compatible roles. If this is the kind of book you want to write, I can advise you only to read the most current ones, and to send for tip-sheets in order to keep up to date with any changing styles - and also to see how smoothly the slightly shifting viewpoint melds in.

But for the beginning writer, keeping strictly to the single-viewpoint narrative keeps the story on a straight and narrow track. It stops the action from jumping from one character to another, making the sequences jerky and sometimes unrelated. This is not to say that there can be no dialogue having arguments. Dialogue in fiction is essential to bring the characters to life, and this point can never be stressed enough.

What single-viewpoint narrative implies, in its simplest terms, is knowing who your story is about, and ensuring that the story is told from her point of view, without deviation, except in minor instances.

Example - single-viewpoint narrative

Margaret picked up the letter from the mat inside the front door.

'It's from David,' she exclaimed. She knew the writing on the envelope instantly, even though it had been three years since she'd heard from him.

'Well, open it, woman!' Frank said.

She looked at him in annoyance, knowing he'd never had much patience with her grief over David's move to Australia, even though he was their only son.

Example - shifting-viewpoint narrative

Margaret picked up the letter from the mat inside the front door.

'It's from David,' she exclaimed.

Frank knew, of course, that she would have recognised the writing on the envelope instantly, even though it had been three years since she'd heard from him.

'Well open it, woman!' he said.

She looked at him in annoyance. He glared back, never having much patience with her grief over David's move to Australia, even though he was their only son.

Again, the purists will say the former scene is the better. I'm honestly not so sure that there's anything so terrible about the second, since it gives a rounded overview of both characters' feelings at that moment. And perhaps this is one of those minor instances when it's preferable to get inside the minds of both characters, since they would both have feelings over the departure of their son. I leave the final decision to you.

THE MULTI-VIEWPOINT NARRATIVE

The multi-viewpoint narrative is the most popular style in long novels of the family-saga type. For many writers, myself included, it is the most satisfying way of writing. It is acceptable to write scenes and chapters from the main character's viewpoint, but it is often desirable to write them from other viewpoints as well. This is something that would be completely out of place in a short story, where the whole thing would simply become muddled. And in shorter novels too, it can become confusing, unless you are an Andrea Newman. But in the blockbuster, almost anything goes ...

But again, know your main characters. Know who your story is really about. It may concern one member of a family or the family as a whole, in which case several narrators in turn may take up the story at different times, in order to give the greatest impact to a scene.

In *The Bannister Girls*, Angel is the central character, but her sisters, her father, and Jacques de Ville, the hero of the novel, all have viewpoint roles, and play their parts as narrators. This kind of writing in a long novel can create depth and texture. The views of the characters can overlap, making them seem more three-dimensional than when they're seen only from a single viewpoint.

The advantages are many. The characters become more rounded when viewed from different angles, both from their own and from other people's. Their innermost feelings can be described by themselves, and can also be seen through someone else's eyes. More sympathy for the characters can be drawn from the reader by these means. But always be careful not to use so many diverse viewpoints that you begin to lose the thread of who is who. Keep control over your storyline, so that one character isn't hogging the limelight too much before you remember that you wanted to use other viewpoints. You may then panic and throw in a whole batch of little cameo scenes from a clutch of viewpoints that will just have the effect of irritating the reader, because by that time, she may be hooked on the major character, whose progress she believed she was following implicitly, and who suddenly seems to have temporarily disappeared while you pursue these other viewpoints.

When you write your chapters, and if you think in scenes as I do, I find it's best to introduce any change of viewpoint with a double double line spacing. The spacing tells you that a change of scene is coming, bringing with it a change of time, setting, angle, or more pertinently in terms of character, a change of viewpoint.

It's essential to let your reader in on who is now taking over the story, because she will still be mentally involved with the character she's been reading about. So, after your double double line spacing, try to begin with the new viewpoint character's name, some dialogue involving him, or some narrative about him. Nothing will madden a reader more than to read half a page about someone whom she thinks is still the same viewpoint character as before only to find she's been reading about someone else.

CHOOSING THE VIEWPOINT CHARACTER

When you write a novel, you will normally have decided very early on who your main character is going to be. In a genre novel, it will be obvious - it will be the romantic heroine, the spy, the detective, the family en masse, the lord of the manor, the unscrupulous landowner, the social climber, the rags-to-riches heroine. You don't have too many problems in deciding whose angle from which to tell your story, whether or not you stick to first person/third person, single-viewpoint or multi-viewpoint narrative.

In this section, I'm concentrating particularly on the way you decide on your viewpoint character in short stories, when you have already chosen a particular theme to write about. The theme I have in mind is that of an elderly lady thinking about joining her son in Australia for an extended visit. To the beginning writer, this would probably mean writing the story from the old lady's point of view. But pause a moment and consider the alternatives. Better than that, read the following examples, and see for yourself how many different ways you could use this theme by choosing a different viewpoint character.

Examples

1.

'Are you all right, ma'am?' The air hostess paused in her flight check, leaning towards the elderly woman clutching her hands tightly over the safety-belt.

Ellen smiled encouragingly at the woman. 'First flight?' she said sympathetically.

'Oh no. But first time to Australia,' Margaret acknowledged.

'You'll be all right as soon as we're airborne and we bring round some drinks,' Ellen told her. 'Everyone feels strange at first. Do you have a family out there?'

'My son. I'm going to stay with him for six weeks. If I like it, I may even decide to stay.'

Ellen didn't miss the pleasure in her voice. Whatever her qualms, she had to admire the old girl for making this long trip. She'd seen plenty of hopefuls going out to Australia in her time, and some of them came back disillusioned. Somewhat cynically, Ellen hoped the son came up to the old lady's expectations.

2.

Margaret checked her safety-belt for the tenth time. It was silly to feel so apprehensive about flying. People did it every day, and planes only rarely fell out of the sky. She wasn't even going to think of hi-jackers ...

She jerked up her head as a voice spoke beside her, and she saw the large male body easing into the sea beside her on the long-haul jet.

'Thank goodness I'm not sitting next to anybody with those headphones permanently attached to their ears,' the voice said pleasantly, and Margaret relaxed a little.

'I could say the same,' she said pertly. She eyed the neat grey hair and smiling eyes above the well-pressed suit of her unknown travelling companion. She wasn't so old that she didn't remember how it felt to flirt a little, and perhaps this long flight to stay with her son in Australia wasn't going to be so boring after all.

3.

Timmy knew he mustn't be tearful, or it was only going to upset Gran. Last night, when she'd read him a bedtime story, she had promised to write to him as soon as she got to Uncle David's house in Australia.

He'd found Australia on the map at school. It looked a very long way away, nearly as far as space, and it was never going to be the same without Gran to run to after school each day. He clung to his mother's hand, wondering if she felt like crying too.

He hated everything about this day. He hated the sounds of the jet engines roaring into the sky every few minutes at the airport, reminding him of why they were here. He hated the way people kept rushing about, nearly knocking him over, and not even saying sorry.

Most of all, he hated the fearful thought that kept creeping into his mind and haunted his dreams, that he was never going to see his Gran again. Things like that happened. In books, they happened all the time.

4.

'You will write straight away, won't you, Mum?' Lynn said yet again as they waited for the flight number to be called. 'We'll all be anxious until we know you've got there all right.' She bit her lip, as Margaret patted her hand.

Their roles might easily be reversed, Lynn thought. Here she was, the capable daughter, wife and mother, holding down a job and running a home, yet she was the jittery one ... While this elegant dowager, more than twice her age, was cheerfully preparing to fly off to the other side of the world as if she hadn't a care in the world.

Why wasn't she the remotest bit scared, Lynn thought with mild resentment? Why couldn't she at least pretend to be sad at parting from her real family, and a bit less eager to visit the renegade son who hadn't been heard of for years?

5.

David tried to assess the spread of his land through his mother's eyes. It was impossible to do, since it would be so alien to anything she knew in the crowded London streets. For a moment he remembered that claustrophobic atmosphere, the pea-soupers in the winter, the street markets, the Cockneys shouting cheery insults to the punters as they sold their wares.

He waited expectantly for the familiar surge of nostalgia, but it no longer came. He stretched comfortably on the porch, knowing that Jilly would soon be bringing out cool drinks before they started the barbie, and the neighbours came round.

How would his mother take to all this, he wondered? To all of it. Australia, the outback, the free and easy life he was so accustomed to now.

Well, he'd soon find out, he thought, with unconscious grimness. The old bird would be arriving on the noon day plane tomorrow, and then they'd just have to see how they got through the next six weeks.

6.

Frank watched his wife mount the steps of the plane with mixed feelings. He was right to let her go. The entire family said so, and Margaret herself had been adamant that he shouldn't go with her.

'We can't afford two fares,' she'd said, always the practical one. 'And besides, you and David - you never really got on, did you? I don't want to spend the next six weeks walking on eggshells between the two of you, and I'll be perfectly all right on my own. It's better that you stay home and mind the shop.'

It was a joke between them. They'd sold the grocery business years ago, but they still referred to either of them being at home as 'minding the shop'. Funny, but until that moment, Frank had forgotten how many times they must have said it over the years.

He suddenly felt his stomach tighten. For God's sake, but he was really going to miss the old girl. The thought hit him with a start of surprise. He'd thought he was going to enjoy this odd feeling of having six weeks' freedom, to go drinking with his cronies, and have a game of darts whenever he wanted to.

Leaving the washing-up until there wasn't a spare bit of room on the draining-board, and having no one to nag at him ... but by all that was holy, he was going to miss her ...

In those six examples you have six embryo stories, each one told by a different viewpoint character, but each using the same basic idea. The resulting stories would also be very different, depending on which narrator you chose to be in control.

CHAPTER 7

CONFLICT AND MOTIVATION

CREATING TENSION
INCREASING AND SUSTAINING SUSPENSE
CONVINCING OPPONENTS
MOTIVATION
AVOIDING CONTRIVANCES
LEADING THE READER FORWARD

CHAPTER 7

In order that characters may progress satisfactorily through the pages of any story, that is, keeping the reader continually interested in their happenings, they are going to have to deal with problems and conflicts.

They may have many mood swings and differences of opinion with other people. They will change their original plans; they will have interrupted conversations; be confronted with sudden and unexpected arrivals, departures and upsets in their lives; face up to the crises of birth, marriage, divorce, deaths; and all the rich tapestry of life that goes on between those states.

If you don't allow them at least some of these things, they will never be the fully realised characters you set out to create. If your characters aren't involved in some kind of conflict, they will be wooden, cardboard, one-dimensional and stilted - all those dreaded and deflating words you don't want to be said about your characters.

CREATING TENSION

The tensions and strains your characters will experience come directly out of the conflicts they encounter. This tension and conflict in your characters can come from many sources. It can come from within the character herself, as she is torn several ways, often by her own conscience. There can be conflict with other characters; conflict with the elements; conflict with politics or the church; physical conflict; or verbal conflict - all of which will produce varying degrees of tension in the mental make-up of the character, and which will affect the way you will write her scenes.

Verbal conflict in fiction is obviously the easiest and most effective way of showing the tension that can exist between people. There's nothing like an aggressive argument in a story for bringing characters vividly to life. Such arguments will reveal their mood at that precise moment, their hurts, frustrations, fears and anxieties. All these things would be brought to the surface in moments of stress, when the tension between the characters would be at its most heightened.

We all say things under stress that we might not normally say. But even more so than in real life, once words have been said in fiction they cannot be taken back, because the words are there in black and white for all to see, and the writer can manipulate their effect in any way that she pleases.

You can allow your characters to retract their vicious words if you will, or to leave their bitterness to damage a relationship to the point of destruction. But the words will still be there on paper, in print, and will never be far from the reader's memory. Cruel barbs from husband to wife - or vice versa - can be a recurring theme in a story about a failing marriage, for instance.

Never be wimpish in your attack on a good argument in a story. Write it as powerfully as you can, with all the emotive words you can command. The strength of a fictional argument simply eludes some people. They make the dialogue far too short, and they are inhibited in the writing, as if their words are practically written in blood and can never be changed.

Never be inhibited when it comes to writing your big argument scenes between your characters. Let it all come out in your first draft. When you read back your scene later, this is the time to tone it down if you feel the need. It may even surprise you to find that it's not quite as daringly dramatic as you thought, and in fact, it pleases you very much as it is.

You may find that the words have lost some of their initial uninhibited impact by the time you read it at this later stage. If you were in the hearts and minds of the characters during their argument, you would have been writing it at the white-heat of their fury, and your words would truly have been *their* words. The scene may not even need to be altered at all, except for minor revising and tidying-up of sentence construction.

A good rousing argument - not necessarily vindictive, but character-revealing - is as good a way of getting under a character's skin as any. And, as in any real argument, as the protagonists get into their verbal stride so their minds roam, bringing out all the nasty little things that have been simmering for some time and which were never meant to be aired, but now come into the open. The tension rises between the two, and you have a powerful scene which thrusts the characters into a new phase of their story.

A well-written argument between characters is never wasted - *provided* it's relevant to the story and not just thrown in for the sake of it. And the relationship between the characters having the argument should be subtly, or blatantly, changed because of it. It may well be strengthened - or it may be doomed for ever.

Creating tension by the use of certain words in the prose and the dialogue is an obvious technique to use. The spy thriller or science-fiction story will use all the pertinent technical jargon to blind the other characters (and often the readers) to what's going on, but the very use of such jargon will heighten the atmosphere and tension between characters. Atmosphere is very important in any story, but it can be created just as easily between the characters' dialogue as in long descriptive passages.

Tension can also be enhanced by the use of short sentences and staccato dialogue, implying shortness of breath, and by the use of carefully chosen, emotive words. In Chapter Two I gave an example of trivial short sentences; these had the irritating effect of holding up the action, rather than moving it forward. But the use of such brief, sharp sentences in an interrogation scene, such as in a war novel or police procedural story, would be valid and necessary to keep up the tension required.

Another area in which dialogue and prose promotes the feeling of tension is in any kind of adventure story. The examples below are from one of my teenage novels - *Anchor Man* (William Heinemann).

In the first scene, the three boys are down a pothole, hopelessly ill-equipped. The dog belonging to one of them has just fallen deeper into the cave system. The tension is still moderately low key at this point. The main character, Jake, is the narrator.

```
    I tried to ignore the painful thumping in my chest as I
moved away from where I had been peering over the edge of
the pothole and sat back on my heels to think.
    Bending my knees like that had made the broken skin on them
tingle, but that was the least of my worries. We were probably
all halfway to getting blood poisoning from all the mud and
dirt we'd crawled through, I thought pessimistically.
    'OK,' I took a deep breath. 'We'll take a vote on it.  Do
we go back and see about getting help, or do we see if we
can get a rope down there and go after him ourselves?'
    'Go down,' Danny stuttered. 'If you say it's all right,
Jake.'
```

```
    'Hawk?'
    'We haven't got much choice, have we?' he said
sharply.
    'Yes we have,' I answered edgily. 'And nobody's moving
a muscle until we're all agreed. Yes or no?'
    'Yes,' he muttered.
    I didn't need telling that he was scared, and so was
I. Very scared.
```

INCREASING AND SUSTAINING SUSPENSE

Later on in the book the tension has increased. In a book of this kind, involving adventure and danger, it's vital to keep up the level of suspense by the increasing sense of terror and fear. Below, is a much later scene. Their imaginations are now playing strange tricks on the boys. Some of the sentences are very short and tight now, causing the reader mentally to pause and take a breath, much as the boys would be doing.

```
    The laughter came again. Above me this time. I swung the
lamp above my head, but there was only the sheer glassy
formation and the gleaming stalactites to be seen. Suddenly
the laughter changed into whispering, unintelligible
gibberish, and I was so terrified I almost dropped my
lamp. I almost hurtled back across the space between me
and the others. At least, it felt as if I hurtled, but
my reactions were so slowed down I probably appeared to
be crawling.
    'Did you hear anything, Danny?' I could feel my lips
shivering now.
    'The water -'
    'No, not the water. Something else.' I didn't want to
put it into words. It sounded so real ... as if we weren't
the only ones down there ...
    'Somebody's laughing?' Danny whispered. 'And talking
daft like Hawk keeps doing?'
    So he had heard it too. It felt as if all my bones were
turning to jelly.
```

'Do you think it's like they hear down the mines, Jake?' he was still whispering, glancing over his shoulder, as if he expected something to leap on him at any minute.

A tiny spark of recollection seeped into my brain from Ron Pearce's book ... if only I could remember. The words wouldn't gel properly in my mind. It was as if I had the book in front of me, the words all dancing about like black dots that wouldn't unravel into coherent shapes until I shut my eyes tightly and forced myself to think.

Then I remembered about 'them'. Strange, imaginary beings that tormented the sanity of anybody who stayed underground too long. I remembered how the book had mentioned them quite coolly and logically, but you had to be down there to appreciate the true horror of 'them'!

The sounds were still incredibly real, even though I knew they were all in my head. And there was all the difference in the world between reading it up in a comfortable room with the telly on in the background, and actually being underground, stiff and cramped and hallucinating, with the terrifying reality of flood water adding to the fear of the unknown.

There are many key words in this last scene to add to the tension and suspense that's being sustained. Whispering; unintelligible; hurtled; crawling; shivering; 'them'; sanity; horror; hallucinating; the contrast between 'coolly and logically' and 'true horror'; the contrast in the last paragraph between the domestic atmosphere of the comfortable room with the telly on, and the reality of the underground cave with flood water rising inside it - all this adds to the tension of the scene. This sentence can be leisurely, depicting the homely atmosphere, while the reader is still fully aware that the reality of the situation is very different. In essence, there's very little description, and all the tension and suspense springs from the reactions of the characters, especially Jake.

The teenage novel of about 30,000 words covered a period of no more than eight hours, and for most of that time the boys were inside the cave, undergoing periods of tension, suspense and despair, while the reader was kept in perpetual doubt as to their hopes of rescue.

CONVINCING OPPONENTS

The conflicts and arguments between the characters in your story must arise from the nature of the characters themselves, and the situations in which you put them. It's pointless having two characters who are so similar in temperament that there will never be a cross word between them.

Sibling rivalry is always a good starting point for conflict in a story. It's natural, and is normally perfectly healthy as the children of different ages in a family develop. But what happens when one member becomes obsessively jealous of another? When one of them has what the other one covets? You should immediately see the possibilities for a tightly plotted story here, with all the involvement of family interests, other members taking sides, the background so familiar in both protagonists, the personalities so intimately known, with all their strengths and vulnerabilities.

An adult novel involving sibling conflict is Frederick Nolan's *Carver's Kingdom*, where one brother, Theo, is described as 'a merchant adventurer, seeker of fortune, builder of empires'; and the other, Ezra, is 'a ruthless manipulator of money and of men, infamous as 'The Black Bay Bastard'. Can't you just see the clashes that are to come - and even without the brief descriptions given, can't you see which is the more upright citizen by the author's choice of names?

A story about twins, one good, one evil, would have a profound effect on a reader. Twins are supposed to be so similar in appearance, outlook, temperament, yet are they always? What if they were separated at birth and brought up in politically, religiously, aesthetically, different environments? Is it logical that their characters would remain similar? I think not.

And what if one twin, an upright Bible-punching school-marm from the Deep South, were to seek out her missing twin, and discover her as a hooker on New York's East Side? It doesn't take much imagination to see where such a split in personality could lead them.

Alternatively, a story involving twins who were similar in every way can have their lives torn apart by wanting the same man, as in Marie Joseph's *Gemini Girls*. Or you could write a story involving a crime, where one twin was mistaken for the guilty one, in which case the external circumstances would be dictating the way your story developed to tear their empathy apart. Would the guilty one confess, or would she let the innocent one take the blame?

Whatever you as author decide to do with your characters, take this message to heart: no conflict, no story.

The opponents in *Anchor Man* were very contrasting characters. They were friends, but, in the competitive way of teenage boys, friendship didn't alter the fact that they became opponents in the book because of their situation. They were three boys of very differing abilities and personalities. The main one was the anchor man, Jake; the other two were slightly simpler characters, Danny and the tough guy, Hawk.

I also chose the names to fit these personalities. Jake is a fairy average name, but still implies some strength by the hard K. Danny has a softer sound; Hawk is much the tougher name with its obvious analogy to the bird of prey. Instant impressions were intended to be given to the reader by the choice of these names.

I deliberately made the boys have differing personalities in order to let them bounce off each other to make the action convincing. There would obviously be arguments and dissension between them. There had to be, or the book wouldn't have worked, and their particular characters were very much an essential ingredient in working out the storyline.

MOTIVATION

The boys' initial motivation in *Anchor Man* to go down the pothole was that of a challenge, a dare, a bet ... all the things likely to concern teenage boys, along with the overriding adolescent need to save face with their peers.

Such motives are a rich source of conflict, tension and suspense when creating characters of any age or status, but teenage characters in particular can run the full gamut, when feelings are at their most intense. Motivation should be a high priority when creating your characters. They should never be allowed to glide smoothly through the pages of your story without giving them reasons for all the things that they do.

Why did your nurse write that poison-pen letter? *Why* was the little boy staring over the edge of the cliff on a Sunday afternoon? *Why* did the gunman feel compelled to burst in on the corporate meeting at that precise time? *Why* did the spaceship commander decide to change course with no *apparent* reason? *Why* did your historical heroine attend the theatre on that particular night? *Why* did the car bomb go off at the wrong time?

The author has to have this initial curiosity about the characters in order to produce the same effect in the reader. We all like to take a look into other people's lives, which is exactly what we do every time we read a novel.

How many times have you glanced into other people's houses, especially through the uncurtained windows at night? I've never yet met the person who hasn't done that at some time! Personally, I find it irresistible. The fiction author never loses that childlike curiosity about people, their surroundings, what makes them tick, and why they do the things they do. That kind of natural, harmless interest will transmit itself to your writing. It will keep it fresh, and keep your characters alive.

Your characters, of course, may not be harmless individuals at all. And your bland, innocent-looking lady peering into someone else's living-room may have more sinister motives at heart. That's fine. You could build your entire story on that one fact alone, providing you give her logical motives for acting the way she does.

If you were writing a story involving any of the above ideas, the reasons for *your* characters doing what they do should be crystal clear in your own mind, even if you don't want to make them instantly clear to your reader *at that point.* I emphasise that comment, because no character's actions should be left totally unexplained for ever. Eventually, you have to come clean, just as the mystery or detective story comes clean at the final showdown when the murderer is denounced.

If a reader reaches the end of a story and is left high and dry as to the reasons for a character's actions, she will feel completely frustrated, if not very angry. Readers' letters might well be sent to the editor, and to take it to extremes, the writer's name may be blacklisted from that magazine or publisher from then on. That is, of course, if your story even reaches publication stage. This in itself is very unlikely, since editors don't have much patience with fictional characters who do things seemingly out of the blue, and even less with the authors who write about them. So be warned.

AVOIDING CONTRIVANCES

The last thing any author wants is for a reader to become exasperated because the characters do things entirely out of context. Readers want a story that's convincing in its plausibility. So suddenly having your hero turning into a computer whiz-kid and solving the entire mystery, when he's been an obvious dummy all through the book, is not going to wash - *unless* he's been hiding his genius all this time for some definite reason of his own, and there have been pointers all through. Then perhaps this final revelation is completely believable.

Avoiding contrivances all comes back to well-thought-through motivation for your characters. Always ask yourself if it's reasonable that your character should act the way he does in certain circumstances. Would he have said the lines of dialogue you're giving him at a certain point in your book? Are you suddenly making him into a caricature figure instead of someone in whom your reader wants to believe totally?

Manipulating your characters into behaving as you want them to in your story is not the same thing as giving them impossible feats to perform and unlikely words to say, either just for effect, or because you can't think of any other way to bring your story to a conclusion.

If you have got to know each character thoroughly before you begin to write, and mentally grown along with them as you write their story, you will automatically reject these false actions. If you do not, think again about your character. Perhaps he's not quite as well rounded in your mind as he should be.

It's worth mentioning the contrivance of putting actual people, whether living or dead, into fictional situations and distorting their persona, their views, their appearances and their locations. At best, you will be destroying your reputation as an author if you start giving someone attributes that other people can immediately identify as false; at worst, you may find yourself at the wrong end of a libel suit. *Do not be tempted to do it!* I would say the only exception to this rule is if you insert an author's note to say why you took liberties with certain events and with certain wordy speeches that would be quite unintelligible to readers. An example where I had to do this in my own work was in *Scarlet Rebel* (Ballantine USA; Severn House) when Charles Stuart landed in Scotland in 1745.

My American editor wanted me to include the prince's actual speech, but on researching it I found it to be so archaic that no one would have been able to read it easily in the novel. I felt that this justified my modernising the speech so that it made sense to readers; and in this case I included an author's note to that effect.

Contrived twists in a plot, and contrived endings to a story, can usually be avoided by asking yourself whether, if you were the character, you would behave in the way you're making your characters behave. If the answer is no, think again. Remember that while your reader is lost in your story, your aim is to make her think that everything that is happening is real.

The characters must seem so real that she can almost touch them; so believable that, depending on which character she's reading about, she's willing them to win through, or to fail, to reach their happy ending or get their come-uppance.

LEADING THE READER FORWARD

This is where motivation in your characters plays an essential part in writing your story. While not being overly concerned with plot in this book, it's reasonable to include the fact that your plot will not exist without your characters having vital motivation for all their actions, and allowing each facet of their behaviour to take them further along the course of your chosen plot.

The main characters will obviously have the strongest motivation for passing from point A to point Z - the parameters of your story. But the assistance they get from their confidante characters, the support group of the minor characters, and sometimes the asides from the walk-ons, will also colour their movements.

In my book, *The Savage Moon*, Rowena Summers, Sphere/Severn House) a walk-on character was essential in leading the reader forward. The main character, Gabe, had written an uninhibited letter, believing he was about to die after injuries sustained in the American Civil War. His letter was to his old sweetheart, revealing his love for her. He never really intended posting it. But an orderly - an unnamed walk-on character - took the letter, assumed it was to be posted, and pushed it into the mailbox.

This simple act led the reader forward into wondering what was to happen next. Was Gabe going to survive? Would Marnie receive the letter? What would be her reactions, and would it result in their getting together after years apart? Since the background of these characters was solid and logical up to this point, the reader would be anxious to know what happened next.

Allowing your characters to read letters in a story is a simple way of leading the reader forward in the action. Letters from one to another can comment on the past, and tell of future happenings, thus sharing the prospect with the reader. There will be the anticipation of what's to come. There may be warnings of danger in the letter. There may be hope, or despair, or sorrow. Above all, there will be information given by the sender, and reactions on the part of the receiver. All of this will produce the curiosity factor that compels the reader to read on. And that's what every author is aiming for.

CHAPTER 8

CHARACTER DEVELOPMENT

KEEPING IT CONSISTENT
FLESHING OUT THE CHARACTERS
THINKING AHEAD
LETTING YOUR CHARACTERS GROW
GETTING RID OF THE UNDESIRABLES

CHAPTER 8

Let's suppose you've thought up an ingenious idea involving a beautiful female spy to decorate the pages of your novel. Or perhaps you have an idea for a story involving a hard-headed racing-car driver. You cannot then sit back and expect either the stereotypes, or the brilliantly unique characters, to write the story themselves without considerable help from you.

It's a fine and wonderful thing to hear an author tell you that her characters become so real to her that they take on a life of their own. To a certain extent they do. The apparent magic of the published author to accomplish this feat is exactly what the beginner envies so much - but however real the characters are to you, you must always be in control, helping them to appear at their best - or their villainous worst.

Face it logically. If characters really took on lives of their own, some would jolly soon reject the dire ending you may have designed for them. They would object to being thrown off a cliff, or being killed off just as they were getting into their most evil stride, or having a love affair with the other woman when she wasn't actually their style at all ...

If you think it's far-fetched that the characters in a story could have this kind of effect on a writer, think about some of the published stories you've read. Haven't you ever become totally impatient with some of the characters, wishing they had done something completely different from the way the author has written about them? Haven't you ever said you would have written that scene differently? If you're an imaginative writer, I'm sure you have.

Even if the published story is perfectly acceptable and well-written, there are still times when another author would have changed things, both in plot and character. And plenty of times when the original author still wishes she could have another go at it when she reads back the published story. Maybe the character doesn't quite gel after all. Her dialogue doesn't come in precisely the way you meant it. Your first choice of adverb has subtly changed your meaning ...

No two people see fictional characters in precisely the same way, any more than our view of the people we meet every day coincides. Since we can't get inside each other's heads, it's an impossibility. And each of us has a slightly different view of the characters we read about. Your view of my blonde bombshell may not be of a woman of the same appearance or temperament as mine. Your impression of my tall, dark villain may not be as tall or as dark or as evil-minded as mine.

The way we create our characters is unique to us. And they must be kept firmly in their place if your story isn't to end up totally in opposition to the way you have worked it out for them. I'm not saying you can't make changes if something terrific suddenly occurs to you during the writing. You always have choices. And very often, it will be *because* your characters have developed so realistically in your mind and on the pages that these changes will become the most brilliant and logical way to continue the story. Just remember who's the boss.

KEEPING IT CONSISTENT

Then comes the hard part. However much you think you know these people to begin with, their appearances, likes and dislikes, and whatever devious plot you've worked out, your characters must develop mentally and *naturally* throughout the pages of your book. They cannot, and should not, remain static.

They may also develop physically. A child will grow into an adult. A young man will eventually turn into a raddled old one. Be aware of the changes you are going to put your characters through, and don't make the mistake of describing each one in exactly the same way on page 350 as you did on page 1. Obvious? Of course. But so easy to forget.

Supposing you begin a story with a guy called Joe, who's been thrown out of the police force for suspected drug-running on the side. Maybe he's just been suspended, which will give the added slant of suspense while the reader waits to know if he's as innocent as he says, despite all the evidence against him.

On page 1 he's as low as he can be, needing to find his self-respect, to say nothing of the respect and support of wife, family, colleagues, friends. You have established a pretty powerful situation, with a character who can be motivated in several different ways.

He can fight to establish his innocence. He can go under, losing everything he once held dear, become a down-and-out, sleeping rough, even succumbing to the drugs he was peddling. He can change his name and take a different job allied with his former profession, such as that of a private eye with a cause, or a score to settle, or as a security man. He can go on the run, hounded by people with a small-town mentality. He may also be suspected of causing a girl's death through the drugs he allegedly sold.

Any of these situations would involve a considerable amount of mental stress for Joe. His character would undergo severe strain, and he might hit rock bottom, but if he is an honest, upright citizen, his basic personality would remain consistent. He would strive against all the odds to prove his innocence, and if this is what you have decreed for him, then as an author, you would be doing him a disservice by portraying him otherwise.

The romantic novel is one area where inconsistency has sometimes been shown up at its worst. The hero who suddenly discovers on the very last page that he's loved the heroine all along, with no realistic indication as to his feeling all through the book, is hopelessly out of date and inconsistent as regards character. If he's been so hateful to her and thought her a silly little twit all through, why on earth should he suddenly think her so wonderful - and, even more to the point, what right-minded modern young woman is going to want him now, after putting up with all his insults?

Always remember how you endowed your characters when you worked out their checklist. Your heroine may have had a jealous streak. Jealousy can be extremely difficult to control, and to a lesser or greater extent I believe it stays with a person all their lives. However well it's kept in check, it can still simmer beneath the surface and explode for the most innocent of reasons. In fiction, jealousy is a very useful character flaw. It can be harmless or totally destructive, arousing amusement in its recipient, or it can have far-reaching and horrendous effects on other people in your story as well as on the central character.

A male character may have been ambitious since adolescence - he could be a City whiz-kid, ruthless to the extent of letting nothing and no one stand in his way. Would he have a change of heart if circumstances dictated it? He may do, but you should still keep that core of strength you checklisted for him, which grew out of his ambition, and that overriding sense of self-confidence that goes with such an obsession.

Your main character may be a child who desperately wanted to ride in the Grand National when she grew up. Who can forget the character Elizabeth Taylor portrayed in the film *National Velvet?* Such an intense focus that you give your main characters is something you must take care not to lose as the story progresses. Otherwise consistency is lost and they are in danger of fading away and turning into the dreaded wimps that nobody admires.

FLESHING OUT THE CHARACTERS

Earlier, I mentioned giving a character her birthday, and not simply saying she was 23 years old in 1962, or whatever. Giving each character her birthday, whether or not I use it significantly in my story, is one of the most simple, yet most effective ways I have found in fleshing out my characters, and then applying all the peripheral things that go with them. I'll explain.

I am an Aquarian, born between 20 January and 19 February. (Actually, 8 February). If I give my female character a similar birthday, even my own, I have an immediate empathy with her. I know how she reacts to different things, because she's more *me* than someone born, say, in the middle of June. While not describing myself as the character, it still gives me the feeling of knowing her from the inside. It works for me, and it may work for you. And naturally, not every character I write about is born in February!

Perhaps you don't give much credence to astrology, but I suspect there aren't many people who don't read their 'stars', even if only to sneer at or ridicule them. And don't we always prefer to believe them when they say you're going to have a good week ... ?

How many times has a person met a new acquaintance, heard something of their views, and asked perceptively 'What's your star sign?' Maybe he seems the ideal Libra subject, whether you consider that character to be sitting on both sides of the fence, or cannily weighing up every angle before making a decision. Or perhaps you suspect he's a prickly Scorpio with his volatile reactions. We're all susceptible to these packaged images, whether we like it or not.

But if Aquarius subjects are reputed to be thinkers, free spirits, intuitive, unpredictable, moody, and so on, then I've got a ready-made idea of how I might define my female character, because I would most likely share those views, or at least some of them. Those who find their fictional characters easy to develop may not find the following ideas necessary to pursue, but for those who find it extremely difficult, it's an option you might consider.

The Aquarian motto is 'I know'. Does this mean she is self-opinionated, or that she would make a good teacher, inquisitive, receptive to and retaining ideas and/or masses of useless information? From the given motto alone, your imagination could start you thinking up ways to flesh out your fictional Aquarian character - even her checklist, which you thought was complete, may have more facets added to it than you thought at first by going to such sources.

Aquarians are reputedly not materialistic, as long as they have enough to live comfortably. They can be impulsive spenders, careless with money, or almost miserly with it. (I am detailing all this objectively, without personal comment!) In one of my contemporary romantic novels, I took many of these ideas further. The heroine was an interior designer who used astrology to suggest colour schemes to fit her clients' personalities. In this case, the heroine came into contact with the wealthy Alex Hart on the island of Jersey, where she was to find that two strong-minded people who shared the same Aquarian passion could frequently clash.

The scene that follows is the first clash between them. The novel was *Enchanted Island* (Jean Innes, Bantam, USA; also featured in *Good Housekeeping* in USA, Spain and Australia).

```
    Shelley felt a sudden thrill. The job was a challenge,
and so was he ... in fact, she hadn't felt so mentally
stimulated for years ...
    'I want the whole place to reflect my personality instead
of my grandfather's,' he said curtly. 'The money doesn't
matter. There's ample, whatever it costs.'
    Shelley gave him the full benefit of her deep blue
gaze. Her heart beat quickly, knowing she was asking for
ridicule, but also knowing she had to ask right now.
    'Would you mind telling me your birth date, Mr Hart?'
    She was right. He stared, his eyebrows rising as if she
was some kind of nut.
```

> 'You have a strange way of changing the subject,' he
> said abruptly. 'Do you want to know my taste in women
> too? For the record, I don't think a lot of any of them
> these days, especially those who ask personal questions
> and poke around in bedrooms on short acquaintance.'
>
> She was full of indignation, and then he gave a small
> shrug.
>
> 'I suppose you'll tell me why you want to know eventually.
> If it's any of your business, Miss Rogers, I'm thirty-
> one years old, and my birthday is February tenth. And
> since we're getting down to basics, I've no intention of
> calling you Miss Rogers for the rest of the day. My name
> is Alex.'
>
> Shelley followed him out of the door. His age was
> immaterial, and she hadn't asked for it. But as for the
> rest ... maybe she should have guessed at once that he
> was an Aquarian, like herself. Their birthdays were only
> two days apart. In many ways, that made her job, according
> to her own astrological ideas if matching a client's home
> surroundings with his zodiac traits, very much easier. She
> knew the Aquarian traits so well ... and that was precisely
> why she knew there would also be plenty of difficulties
> ahead with Alex Hart.

My book using the zodiac idea was a one-off in 1982. There has also been a series of novels on both sides of the Atlantic using the theme of mixing birth signs referring to characters.

THINKING AHEAD

Give your characters their birth dates with a view to thinking ahead in your story. You might also use the old rhyme of *Monday's child is fair of face, Tuesday's child is full of grace* to further the persona of your character. Everything adds to your own perception of your fictional character, which should be every bit as complex as a real person.

If the heroine of your historical novel is approaching her eighteenth birthday, for instance, this can produce a birthday ball; a coming-of-age party; a coming-out ball; or an inheritance. This in turn can affect other members of the family circle.

The inheritance idea is where you often need to think ahead. Plan your characters within your story plan so that the correct terms apply to them when a death occurs, or a character approaches the age when a bequest becomes due. Plan a mixture of ages, infirmities, peculiarities and whatever else is needed to produce this mixture of people, and the possibilities for future events.

In a family saga, it's a good idea to draw out the family tree of the characters for their own reference. Claire Rayner actually included a fictional family tree in the frontispiece of her novel *Soho Square*, as well as in other books. It showed readers the cast of main characters at a glance, and subtly led them into half-knowing them already, and into being curious as to the interrelationships that would occur in the book.

LETTING YOUR CHARACTERS GROW

No characters should remain static throughout the course of a story. Whether the aim of the author is to portray an incident in a short story, or to write an epic novel on a worldwide scale, the characters involved in that story must move forward in stature, in thought, in age and circumstance.

In a story covering years, your characters will grow physically. They will grow older; therefore they will grow taller, thinner, fatter, heavier, and so on. Their hair will change colour, not always naturally; it may become grey or white; thin, or non-existent.

All these things are obvious external ways to let our characters grow and change in the eyes of the reader. But they may be allowed to grow only in mental attitude as did my boys in *Anchor Man*. After all, they were only eight hours older at the end of the book, than they were in the beginning, but they had undergone vast changes in mental attitude by then. In many ways, they had grown up.

How they grow depends largely on the characters you are writing about. But to allow them to develop in this way during the pages of your story, you should be asking yourself questions about them.

How would they cope with the many crises we all have to face in life? How would they react facing up to grief, to coming across a road accident in which their own child or parent was involved? How would they face sudden success, or wealth, or the prospect of a terminal illness? Would they cope well with birth, marriage, divorce, death, addiction, broken relationships?

The strength of your characters can be brought out in many situations, but only you can decide how you will let them grow out of whatever fate throws at them. And since you decide that too, it's quite a burden you take on.

GETTING RID OF THE UNDESIRABLES

By undesirables, I mean all the characters you need to dispose of in any story, not necessarily by killing them off, but by letting them out of the plot logically and efficiently.

Some people find it extraordinarily difficult to rid themselves of some of their characters. They seem to cling like leeches, with a mention of every last one of them to round off a story. That may be perfectly feasible in a family saga, when each member may need to play his part in rounding off the story. But in many stories such crowded scenes simply hinder and divert the real *raison d'être* of the central characters.

Throughout the story there can be many times when you don't want characters to keep cropping up and you need to get rid of them, whether for a short time or permanently. Children can be sent off to boarding school, or sent abroad, or to live in another part of the country with relatives. People will get married and move away. They may join a kibbutz or take up a job in America, or they will simply have served their purpose in the story and be allowed to drift out of it smoothly and efficiently. You simply cannot have every character you first thought of on stage all of the time.

Many times you will need to let a character die. You may have become very fond of this character, and are loth to let him go. You linger over his deathbed scene lovingly, when perhaps he really needed to be got rid of in a much tighter scene to allow the stars to move on. A death scene is also always a good way to show the reactions of other characters.

Try to be objective as you re-read the way you write such scenes, and be objective also about the way other authors have done it. But remember always to be ruthless in removing those characters who are no longer important to your story, and know when to make it a lengthy scene or a short, sharp one.

In *The Bannister Girls*, a death scene occurs when the chauffeur of the family is brought back on a stretcher at the railway station where Angel and her mother are offering tea and sympathy to the returning wounded. This demanded some poignant detail, since he had been part of their lives for a long time. Lady Bannister has been doing this work for some time, but it's Angel's first experience of the results of war.

> 'Miss Angel, is that you?'
> She blinked, startled by the poor wretch on the stretcher. The blanket had been pushed away from his body by his restless clawing in the air. He had no legs below the thighs, and his head rolled from side to side as if eternally trying to see or hear something beyond his reach. His eyes were swollen, bloodshot and glazed in his parchment face, and the orderly with him shook his head slightly at Angel, who reeled back with absolute shock.
> 'Oh - Hobbs! Oh my God - oh Hobbs, it's you!'
> Her voice was high and choking and filled with anguish as her mind almost refused to believe what she was seeing. Such a little while ago Hobbs had left their employ, to go chirpily to war, bragging about all the French mamselles he was going to charm. Now he was no more than a broken shell of a man, and clearly with so little time left on earth. And Angel just couldn't bear it … she just couldn't ...
> 'Hobbs, how simply wonderful to have you home again.' Clemence pushed past her. 'You'll drink a cup of tea, won't you?'
> Her mother knelt down in the dust so that her face was level with Hobbs' beside the stretcher. She gently held up the chauffeur's head with one hand while touching the cup to Hobbs' lips with the other. She did it all with as much finesse as though she was dispensing tea from their own silver teapot, ignoring the fact that most of the tea dribbled instantly down Hobbs' chin as tremors shuddered through him.

> 'Where will he be taken?' Clemence asked. The orderly lifted his head as if to say it didn't really matter, and the Bannister women watched their chauffeur being carried away, knowing it would be the last they ever saw of him. Angel felt her mother's hand grip her shoulder.
>
> 'There are others who need help, Angel,' Clemence said quietly, and turned immediately to the next man. Angel saw the strength in her mother's elegant shoulders, and somehow smothered her own terror to carry on.
>
> The afternoon had been a revelation to her. Had she once imagined blithely that she could be a nurse? She had never given a single thought to what it really entailed. She had perhaps romantically visualised for a few moments the glory of tending a patient, of receiving adoring glances and smiling thanks from those she had helped to heal ...
>
> She had never once considered the open suppurating wounds or the recurring nightmares after the terror of being gassed, or the cauterising and disposal of amputated limbs. She hadn't known the appalling sweet heavy smell of blood ... There was so much she didn't know, and never before had she felt so ignorant nor so helpless.

While removing the character Hobbs, note how he finally becomes referred to as the chauffeur, how the orderly (the walk-on) is unnamed, and how Angel and her mother are referred to as the Bannister *women* in the relevant paragraph, which subtly dignifies them at that moment. The entire sentence is shaded and solemnised by having no reference to individual names, and it becomes more emotive because of it.

But not every death scene has to be sombre; there can be a kind of humour, even something approaching slapstick. The news of her husband's death as reported to Louise Bannister Crabb produced a very different reaction to the one quoted above. Louise is the married sister in *The Bannister Girls*, and normally the most correct and restrained; but sudden shock can turn even the most conventional mind, as in the scene below. There's no dialogue in this scene, nor any real sense of grief. Louise's totally unexpected reactions, and that of the officers, were intended to be all the more farcical by evoking visual images alone, and I offer it without comment.

Louise wept into her lace-edged handkerchief, sick to her stomach at realising that the feeling she felt most was the most acute, yet appalling sense of relief. The officers cleared their throats and murmured comforting platitudes, one of them daring to put an arm around the grieving young widow and sensing the tautness of her supple body.

Poor young woman, he thought sympathetically. But a handsome one too. Perhaps in time she would find someone to take the place of that pompous Crabb fellow. An officer and a gentleman, Stanley certainly was, but the general opinion of him was that he was the most boring bore in the British Army.

Snuffling into her lace handkerchief, Louise couldn't shake off the image of Stanley being blown to bits. But it was not in the least like the embarrassed officers imagined.

She was seeing Stanley's arms and legs flying off in four directions. His head shooting upwards, the eyes still slightly surprised and affronted at what was happening, the fleshy mouth hanging open in that stupid vacant way of his. And then there was that other bit in the middle. That ridiculous, flaccid appendage that rarely stood up straight like a little soldier the way it was supposed to, and was probably filling up with pee as it wobbled about, showering everybody around him ...

Louise, who hardly ever let such coarseness enter her mind, let alone pass her lips, was suddenly giggling wildly at the thought of dear departed Stanley's penis suddenly having a life of its own and peeing over everything in sight.

CHAPTER 9

VISUAL
WRITING

PERSONALITY-PLUS
COLOURFUL CHARACTERS
MORE VISUAL IMAGES
BODY LANGUAGE
MATERIAL TRAPPINGS
MAKING CHARACTERS COME ALIVE

CHAPTER 9

Louise's scene from *the Bannister Girls*, quoted in the previous chapter, was deliberately intended to jolt and amuse, both by the unexpectedly frank descriptions in the mind of the so-correct Louise, and by the visual pictures it put into readers' minds.

Her fantasy wasn't all that terrible, but since the words were supposed to be in Louise's head at that moment, it was still much further than a prim and proper young lady of the period would go. Her reactions were also intended to break the mould of what can inevitably become a rather depressing monotony of dramatic death-scenes during a war novel.

Visual writing is an author's most powerful asset. Making your readers see your characters, with as few words, or as emotive a description as possible, is what we should all be striving for, all the time. But that's not to say there can be no lovely descriptions of people or places. What it means is that you discard the weak words you may have first thought of, and learn to use the most effective ones you can to conjure up these pictures in the mind.

It's a technique that comes with practice, but is worth every bit of revision you consider necessary. Eventually, you will find you are automatically thinking of visual words for fiction, rather than the everyday ones we all use.

I don't advise revisions just for the sake of it, or because someone else has told you how many times they revised *their* book, making you feel inadequate because you've only checked yours through once ... Of course, you need to read through your story, checking for typing errors, spelling mistakes, punctuation, sentence construction etc., but revision doesn't necessarily mean cutting. Sometimes it means expanding to make your meaning absolutely clear. I think it's a mistake to overdo ruthless revision to the point of leaving nothing of substance in the writing.

But that is an overall view of your work. When it comes specifically to characters, it pays to take time in asking yourself if a particular word or phrase is really the most potent one you can find to make them vividly alive. Always strive to use the most visually appealing words you can to describe those characters, words that will refine and underline their personalities to get the most out of them for your readers.

PERSONALITY-PLUS

Years ago this is what used to be called 'oomph'. Before that it was simply 'it'. More recently it was called 'charisma', and yet more basically, 'sex appeal'. Whatever it is, the fortunate people who have it are those who immediately stand out in a crowd because of that indefinable, elusive quality we call personality. It's not always easy to know what it is that gives one person such a plus-factor over another, but it's an enviable quality in real life, and in fiction.

Who could recall John Mortimer's Rumpole without hearing him refer in his larger-than-life manner to 'She Who Must Be Obeyed'! Would Rumpole be half as eccentric a character without that ponderous manner and pertinent turn of phrase that Mortimer bequeaths on him?

And what a magical name he chose. Rumpole ... unable to be said without emphasis on the first syllable, rolling off the tongue, halfway to being rumbustious, which is exactly what the character is. And how cleverly that reference to the lady indoors defines both their characters in one simple phrase. Would it have been half as emotive if he had merely said 'the wife'?

Personality-plus doesn't always come from eccentricity, but it certainly helps. Picture the vicar with the penchant for always speaking in clichés and in sepulchral tones to match his calling; the teenager who can't think without having headphones attached to her ears; the would-be spy who advertises his presence by his tendency to drop vital spying equipment from his person at inopportune moments; the burglar who frequently forgets his tools; the old lady with a nice sideline in book-making among the quiet neighbours; the Jekyll-and-Hyde personality.

But what of the rest? What of those who don't have a specialised job or disposition that helps them lean towards eccentricity? How do you make them characters to remember, the ones that linger in the mind long after the story has been read?

Each author has her own idea of what makes an ideal fictional character, whether it's in a tense story about the Mafia or a gentle meandering romance. In the first type of story, it's easy enough to imagine a vicious thug, cold-bloodedly getting rid of everyone who stands in his way ... in the other, it's not so easy to make a seemingly average woman stand out in a crowd and become special. She has to have something that will lift her out of that crowd. Some special skill, perhaps, that is only apparent when danger strikes. It may be calmness when everyone else is going berserk, coupled with an ability to talk the thugs out of their evil intent; she may have a mastering of a foreign language that may not be the one the hijackers are using but which is intelligible enough to allow her to act as interpreter in a tense situation when everyone else is helpless.

There are any number of ways in which you can promote your average character to one of stature and personality, especially when he is fighting against his own instincts to do whatever you have decreed for him. Your hero may be the only driver around when a child needs taking to hospital. Does he really want to take on the responsibility? Won't he miss the all-important interview if he does? So what will be his decision?

Remember the old cowboys and Indians again. How many times did we see the Indian child become ill or injured, and, surprise, surprise, the captured white man is the only one with the knowledge and skill to save him? He will be killed if he lets the child die, and he will be raised in stature if he saves him. The character's tension, motivation and strength of personality are all involved in that one small situation, even though we all know which way the story will go.

COLOURFUL CHARACTERS

In basic terms, the use of colour when describing your characters is something to be considered carefully. Cornflower-blue eyes have become something of a genre cliché that is best avoided.

Some novelists describe their characters with no more than the barest mention of colour, either in clothes or personal accoutrements, leaving all to the imagination of the reader. I think this is a pity. Most readers need, and appreciate visual descriptions.

For me, trying to see characters with no colourful descriptions at all would be like watching a film on television in black and white, or rather, in dull shades of grey. Turning up the colour is a great relief, and the characters suddenly come to life. Colour is a wonderful aid to showing your character's personality, so use it wisely.

If you discover that the girl on the black and white TV screen was actually wearing a scarlet dress, it may alter your impression of her entirely, if you'd been wondering for ten minutes whether it was blue or yellow or green. So the man wore a bright blue suit, instead of the conventional dark grey you'd imagined. Don't these new images immediately change your interpretation of the people who would be wearing these more extrovert colours?

Red is generally accepted as being a hot colour, blue as cool. Green is calming, yellow is the sunshine, look-at-me-I-want-to-be-noticed colour. Orange is violent, brown is of the earth, safe and controlled. Therefore someone who always dresses in shades of beige and brown, the earth colours, would be seen as a person of a more retiring nature. The understatement of black and white on a dazzlingly beautiful professional model with glowing auburn hair would have a dramatic effect. Use all the subtle shades in the artist's palette to vary the way you describe your colours. Tawny browns, amber, ultramarine, crimson, gold...

Use colour to every advantage, and use texture too. Shiny clothes say something about the wearer, as do the use of sequins and gilt trimmings and rich velvets. Cheap cotton underwear, or expensive silk, says still more. A man in a dark trenchcoat may just be cold, or he may be hiding behind its impersonal appearance.

Colourful characters can be interpreted in another way, not just because of the colours they chose to identify their personas, but because of their lifestyles. They can be the type beloved of romantic novelists, from the sheikhs in their billowing white robes shown to magnificent effect against their naturally dark or tanned skins - Lawrence of Arabia is still a dashing hero to many - to the flamboyant and daring pirates still flourishing in many American novels. Descriptions of these types can be blatantly written, since the aim is to get them visually in front of the reader in the most direct manner.

In *Moonlight Mirage* (Sally Blake, Futura/FA Thorpe), Marianne is such a character, now disguised as a Tunisian concubine. The writing style is frank and sexy, going straight for the senses:

> On her wrists and arms were placed silver armlets, barbaric in design as befitted the concubine of a prince ... around her neck hung silver chains with matching anklets above her feet. Marianne gasped at the voluptuous vision who stared back at her from the looking-glass.
>
> It was like looking at a stranger. A very beautiful stranger, with the gossamer garb, the colour of Islam, suggested by Dominic himself ... Her hair, burnished to the colour of chestnuts, and her skin so dark and glistening. The unexpectedness of her blue eyes and the fine European contours of her face, that no amount of make-up could disguise, gave the effect of blatant sensuality.

MORE VISUAL IMAGES

The small scene described is intended to make you see Marianne as clearly as Dominic sees her. If you have a hard time thinking up a variety of strong and visual words to bring the imagery of your characters to life, the value of a good thesaurus cannot be emphasised enough. It should be your constant companion, as it is mine.

Compare Marianne's sensual description with the more comical one of Thomas Finley, who appears in my *All In The April Morning* (WH Allen/Star). The use of colour is still to the fore:

> Bridget's first impression was that he reminded her of one of the bawdy music-hall acts in newspaper pictures. Thomas Finley was large and broad, with mutton-chop whiskers in a florid face, and tufty brown hair on top of his head.
>
> The hair was so dense in colour that Bridget was sure it must be dyed, because it contrasted so starkly with the corrugated face. His suit was of a very loud check pattern of pale beige and green, and his fingers glittered with rings. He was in such complete contrast to his austere sister that Bridget and Kitty could only stare at this comic vision.
>
> 'So you're our protégées, are you?'
>
> They stared dumbly, not understanding the word. Thomas Finley's eyes were pale grey like his sister's, but that was the only similarity. Bridget didn't like his eyes.

> When he wanted to hide his feelings, they were completely devoid of expression. It was a weapon Thomas frequently used in business dealings.
>
> 'Do you have tongues in your heads?' His smile revealed uneven, discoloured teeth. He made no attempt to hide his own accent. It was strident and broad. He came to the front of the desk and perched on the edge, supremely self-confident, his patent leather two-tone shoes the latest thing, adding to the image of the showman.
>
> 'Yes, of course, we do,' Bridget said.
>
> 'And you, child?'
>
> 'Yes sir, Mr Finley,' Kitty stammered. He laughed, reaching forward to tickle her under the chin. He smelled of scent. Their daddy always said they should never trust a man who wore scent. He moved back and sat behind the desk again, his arms spread out as if he encompassed the world.

The first part of this scene, describing Thomas's apparel, makes him seem as bland as the circus clown he appears to the young girls. But later on, the more sinister side of his character is quickly revealed by the more personal reference to the man himself. Colour is very much an asset to this scene. The tufty dense brown hair, bright clothes, the Hollywood gangster two-tone shoes, the pale grey, cold eyes, the discoloured teeth. And finally, as a complete contrast, another sense is brought in, the smell of scent on a man, so abhorrent to the girls. It's not hard to see he's already damned in their eyes.

BODY LANGUAGE

If you 'saw' how Thomas Finley perched on the edge of his desk, and then seated himself behind it, using his arms in various ways while he towered over the young girls coming under his control, then you were aware of body language. This is extremely useful in letting your characters underline their personalities.

The bank manager will sometimes use the techniques ascribed to Thomas Finley. So will the army sergeant or other interviewer, intent as he is on letting the timid new recruit be sure who is in charge of the situation.

Watch any two people in a restaurant and assess their relationships from their body language. Young lovers will lean forward across the table, almost oblivious to their food, gazing into each other's eyes unblinkingly. They are open and uninhibited in their affection. They may or may not need words. They may be dressed boldly, or in casual jeans and sweatshirts, confident enough not to need flamboyant outward trappings.

The older married couple will sit back in their chairs; her arms may be demurely on her lap, her hands probably loosely clasped; his arms may be folded as they await the food which will give them a topic of conversation. They look around the room, examining other people, the décor, other people's food choices. She will wear a tidy dress, he will wear a suit.

The business couple of opposite sexes meeting for the first time will have dressed carefully to impress. They will assess each other carefully, with polite quick smiles and controlled dialogue. He will order good wine which he will taste before allowing the waiter to pour it. She will sip confidently.

The business couple of the same sex will behave differently. Two men who know each other will produce occasional loud laughter, sharing in-jokes, each one probably trying to outdo the other. Their body language will also produce a leaning forward over the table, and frequent eye contact, an air of camaraderie. If they are strangers the mood will be changed. One will inevitably try to dominate the other, by smiles that may be frank or secretive, by familiarity with the menu, the waiter, with others in the restaurant. If one is desperately trying to win the other's confidence, he will defer to him by asking his opinion on the food, the choice of wine, and by saying how much he has wanted this meeting. His hands will be spread in an open manner while he is saying such things, implying that he has nothing to hide. This can be a useful ploy to use in a story when your character has everything to hide.

Two women dining together may have very different body language. Businesswomen may well dress to kill, again with the need to impress and dominate. Eye contact may be very little, as each tries to see what effect this meeting is having on other people. They may smile a lot, but the smiles may well be guarded.

If they are there for the sole purpose of being seen, as would be certain stars of stage or screen, their whole attitude will be exaggerated and flamboyant. They may complain loudly to the waiter, commanding his attention and, in doing so, drawing attention to themselves.

Mother and daughter dining out can have different roles, depending on the situation. If confident daughter is taking mother out, she will be in control. Her actions will be quicker, more confident. She will read the menu, probably aloud, and she will order the food, then put down the menu and smile into her mother's eyes. Inside, she is still the small girl, out to impress, in effect saying, 'There, aren't I clever, Mother?'

If mother is in control, daughter may well be embarrassed at being in the restaurant at all. Or she may be wishing herself somewhere else. She may be fidgeting with her hair, or the edge of the tablecloth, while mother glances at her impatiently from time to time as she orders the food for them both.

A clandestine pair of lovers will sit as closely as possible. If they cross their legs, the whole shift of the body will be towards each other, shortening the distance between them. The shoulders will be relaxed, the fingers curling around a wine glass, though they seem hardly to notice if they are drinking or not.

If you think any or all of these situations are stereotyped or produced solely for the purposes of this chapter, you're wrong. They are all people I have observed. I've noted down their actions in a notebook afterwards - not at the time, I hasten to say, or I might have been accused of being an undercover agent or something. It's a good exercise to be an observer of body language, because we all use it. It's the game we all play, whether we're conscious of it or not. And it's a very useful trick to remember when you describe the way your characters are behaving with one another.

MATERIAL TRAPPINGS

The material trappings and accessories with which you surround your characters will also say a great deal about them. Does she wear glasses? Are they vitally necessary for her to be able to see? Or are they fashion accessories, with large coloured frames? Are they studiously horn-rimmed, half-glasses, flamboyant, rimless, tinted? Simply saying that a character wears glasses leaves half of his personality out. By the addition of no more than an extra word or two you can influence your reader's reception of your character.

Apart from the colours of the clothes your characters wear, the style of clothes will say a great deal about them. Think of the woman in the tailored business suit; the fussy, meticulous dresser - man or woman; the floral summer dress; the frills; the preference for trousers as opposed to skirts.

Does your female character wear hats - small, large, fussy, always, sometimes, never? Does she always wear the same identifiable perfume, or does it change with her mood? Does she hate artificial scents of any kind?

What about her jewellery? Does she prefer pearls to glitter? Long earrings to studs? An ankle chain? A bold mannish watch with a clear dial, or a glittery diamante-studded affair with figures so tiny they can hardly be seen?

Shoes next. Maybe she's wearing brogues, or teetering high heels; suede flatties, sandals, or cowboy boots. Don't you have a different idea about the wearer of each of these types of shoes? You should do, if your imagination is working in fictional terms.

Perhaps your male character is wearing a uniform. This usually gives him immediate stature and identification, whether he's an army captain, a police inspector or a traffic warden.

Does your male character have a tattoo, or other distinguishing mark? Does he have a mole on his forehead; different coloured eyebrows; a limp; a shifty way of walking? He may be clean-shaven, sprout a full moustache, a pencil-thin one, or one with waxed tips. He may have a full beard, a skimpy one, or a carefully shaped one.

He may have a pet. A cat-lover will instantly portray a different impression from a man who owns a Rottweiler. A female character with a fluffy blue Persian cat may automatically make your reader think, however wrongly, that the owner of such a cat is also a bit fluffy and therefore scatter-brained. It's strange, but true, that we see ourselves in relation to the things with which we surround ourselves.

Make use of all the accessories you can, including the food and drink your character prefers. I'll leave all the variations on such a vast subject as that to your imagination.

MAKING CHARACTERS COME ALIVE

All of the above should have given you some idea of the endless task we undertake in creating fictional characters out of the air. It shouldn't be minimised, but nor should the enormous enjoyment and satisfaction we derive when readers tell you how well they 'knew' those characters in your latest book.

But the net grows still wider in terms of material trappings. However well you have described the personal appearance of your characters, dressed them and decked them out in jewels and perfumes and surrounded them with hamsters or guinea pigs or pure-bred Arabian horses, you still don't know everything about them.

There are thousands of different professions and lifestyles you can give your characters, and one of the major accessories that goes with them is the car they drive. Or maybe they don't drive. Your hero may be a motorcycle enthusiast, or a keen cyclist. Your heroine may walk everywhere, for the exercise. But a car is said to be second only to a man's wife in terms of pride and value, so whether he drives an ancient Rolls-Royce or a souped-up Mini obviously says a great deal about him.

He may be restoring a vintage car, in which case a sense of loving care and patience will be conveyed about him before you say anything else. He may own a sporty little red two-seater, which will give a different impression.

Many fictional TV characters have their own distinctive cars. Bergerac is a case in point. You only have to see his distinctive maroon Triumph Roadster inching around the Jersey byways to know who's behind the wheel. The car becomes part of the man.

The profession you give your character obviously defines him still further, and so does the home in which he lives. Fictional characters don't, and shouldn't, live in a vacuum. They have lives beyond the vivid incidents and events you're depicting in your story. As well as the dramatic crises you will put them through, they will have a front door to call their own, through which the other characters in the story may or may not go, but which you as the author, certainly will.

It all comes back to that vicarious delight we take in glimpsing into other people's lit living-rooms. Or the fascination in the TV programme *Through The Key-Hole*, where we all try to guess who lives in a house like *that*! Could that clinically tidy place possibly belong to the scatty pop star with the wild hairstyle? Do worldwide travellers really collect such masses of exotic memorabilia and/or unbelievable tat, and have such a clutter in every room and on every surface?

There's an inquisitiveness in all of us, and no less in the reader of a short story or novel, who wants to know exactly what that kitchen and living-room looks like.

Is your reluctant housewife character adept in sweeping everything under cushions when unexpected visitors come to call? Is that fragrant scent of air-freshener really intended to hide the smell of burnt cooking in that catastrophe of a kitchen? Are those books alphabetically arranged on the bookshelves, library style? Or are they stacked anywhere, regardless of importance or size? And what do either of those statements say about the owner of the books?

And what about those black silk sheets and mirrored ceiling in the bedroom ... ? Well, I'll leave you to decide what they have to say about their owner.

I mentioned a notebook earlier, and I do think this is an essential part of a writer's equipment. You should become a collector of snippets of information as they occur to you, for if you don't write them down at the time, they will probably be forever lost to you - at least, they will never be as intense as they first appeared in your mind.

A fleeting impression, a passing scent, a colour, an emotive sound, a gesture - all of these, and many more of the innumerable facets that go to make up the human condition, can be recorded in your notebook, and used later to help bring to life the fictional characters that exist in your head. It's truly a magical moment when that character comes alive for you, because this is the first step in making him come alive for your readers.

CHAPTER 10

GETTING THE HUMAN APPEAL

READER-CHARACTER IDENTIFICATION
WRINGING THE EMOTIONS
CHARACTERS IN LOVE
CHARACTERS AT WAR

CHAPTER 10

Stories are about people, and the most elaborately worked-out storyline is not going to be successful unless your readers can identify with your characters in some way. To get a shared involvement in the story from your reader, they must be given characters for whom they can feel some emotion, whether it's love, hate, grief, sympathy, triumph, and so on.

However fantastic the story may be - perhaps it's one involving beings from outer space or other worlds - the characters portrayed must still have the human values which we all understand.

ET became a loveable creature and almost a cult figure because of his human appeal. Didn't we all, in the end, come to have a strange kind of affection for the Daleks in *Doctor Who*, even though we were so terrified of them in the beginning? And even while we were feeling that terror, they appealed to our human instincts because they were the unknown, and the unknown always tends to instil a sense of fear in us.

But the trick of humanising all those alien beings we find in science-fiction stories is not done just for the sake of it. Bringing human attributes into the unknown also serves to create a comforting human image in something that would otherwise be a frightening and alien thing.

There's also the comic relief value of bringing aliens metaphorically down to earth, in giving them squeaky voices, or letting them be accident prone, or talk with a lisp or a stutter. In the midst of the alien world inhabited by some of these fictional beings emerge the familiar human frailties, and suddenly we are not so afraid. These are things we know and understand, because they're the stuff of us all.

If you create a detective hero who has no human failings, or flaws, no family background, no interest in girls, stamps, boats, hobbies or whatever, you create a cardboard figure. He is one-dimensional, and no reader will be as interested in him as she will be in one who has inner worries about his wife's health, or getting to the local football match on Saturday, even while he's in hot pursuit of a criminal.

Any such diversion in his mind would at least make the automaton of your detective character human. None could be more downbeat in appearance and full of irritating mannerisms than Lieutenant Columbo, with his terrible old raincoat and constant asides. But his character sticks in the mind, and his personality is enhanced because of these things.

None of us is exclusively devoted to one topic at a time. Our brains carry a vast amount of information in them, so that while we're doing one thing, we are often thinking of another. We are able to perform our everyday tasks on more than one level of consciousness. So can your characters - though not to the extent that every scene is a muddle of their thought processes and/or dialogue. But be aware of this fact, and don't let your character, however ruthless or self-centred, be so narrowly focused that he cannot think of more than one thing at a time. Your characters will be seen to be far more human, if they act in a realistically human way.

It goes without saying that readers will be willing on the central characters in your story to do whatever you have planned for them. Don't disappoint them. Let your characters realise their full potential in terms of the hero winning the girl; the spy-ring being cornered by the clever cop; the Mountie getting his man; the prisoners of war making their triumphant escapes; the rags-to-riches heroine achieving her goals by her own magnificent efforts; the daredevil James Bond clone risking his all to thwart his evil enemy.

READER-CHARACTER IDENTIFICATION

There are many well-known quotations and proverbs that can make wonderful starting points for creating your characters. All of them refer to people and/or some aspect of human behaviour, thus giving instant reader-identification.

Hell hath no fury like a woman scorned, for instance. We hardly need telling what the fictional character based on this quotation would be like.

I once heard a superb variation on this theme, with the saying that no enemy is as vindictive as a former best friend. This is a wonderful quote to go into a writer's notebook, and is included in mine. It could conjure up all kinds of possibilities for characters with whom almost everyone could identify; after all, which of us has never been let down by a friend? You may think this is a strange, pessimistic remark, but I'd say that only the most fortunate among us could truly deny it.

I'm not suggesting that we all have treacherous friends of the very worst variety. (With friends like *her*, who needs enemies - to use another well-worn quote!) The let-down may be very minor - a friend who can't keep an appointment for a perfectly genuine reason, but who nevertheless disappoints us; the promise to look after the cat and feed the goldfish while we're on holiday that falls down because the offerer is on holiday at the same time. Or it may be the ultimate in many women's eyes; the treachery of a best friend who steals another's man.

Some authors use proverbs for plotting purposes or titles, but they can also trigger off ideas for characters. I offer a selection below, together with my own ideas as to how I might use each proverb to give me a starting point when I was looking for a character to write about, who may or may not turn out to be a main character.

- **Fools rush in**
  A set of 'crazy gang' characters in a spoof story.
- **Appearances can be deceptive**
  A baby-faced hijacker, or someone in disguise.
- **Beauty is in the eye of the beholder**
  A character facing up to disfigurement in a partner.
- **Blood is thicker than water**
  Characters involved in family loyalties.
- **Blood will always tell**
  A character forced to accept his past - or his future responsibilities.
- **Cheats never prosper**
  A rogue getting his comeuppance.
- **Children and fools tell the truth**
  A child inadvertently reveals a family secret; or a careless character gives away some important secret.
- **When in doubt, do nowt**
  An indecisive character, sitting on the fence at important moments.
- **The grass is always greener on the other side of the fence**
  An envious, covetous character; or someone dissatisfied with their present circumstances.
- **Hope springs eternal**
  A lovely, bubbly, optimistic type of character.
- **Life begins at forty**
  A lively female, throwing off the restraints of her old life, and having a high old time with a toyboy!
- **Look before you leap**
  An impulsive character, always getting in hot water.

- **Love me, love my dog**
  Selfish, opinionated, mother's boy.
- **Lucky at cards, unlucky in love**
  The gambler, risking all on the turn of a card, and losing all he holds dear in the process.
- **Money talks**
  He has it, she wants it, and agrees to marry him to get her greedy little hands on it.
- **Never too old to learn**
  The mature student, having a high old time with the younger students, and the repercussions that follow.
- **Old sins cast long shadows**
  Family feuds coming back to haunt the present generation ... or the sins of the fathers coming home to roost.
- **Pity is akin to love**
  The soldier's sweetheart prepared to marry her wounded hero, even though she's found someone else in the meantime ...
- **Politics make strange bedfellows**
  Intrigue in parliamentary circles, with two men - or women - in a power struggle.
- **Silence means consent**
  A rape victim.
- **Stolen fruit is sweet**
  A wife or husband caught up in an affair and torn between loyalty and love.
- **Time is a great healer**
  A woman coming to terms with the loss of husband, child or lover.
- **He travels fastest who travels alone**
  The loner in whatever setting you choose.
- **Even a worm will turn**
  The nagged husband, wife or colleague, finally being driven to kill.
- **Power corrupts**
  A sinister character, intent on taking over a corporation, no matter how he does it, or who he walks over and ruins in the process.

These are only a few suggestions of the ways you could interpret each proverb; there would be many alternative themes. But when you're stuck in finding that particular human appeal you want to give your characters, it's an exercise that may well pay dividends. Something as simple and intriguing as browsing through a book of proverbs and quotations can start you off with some wonderful ideas for characters.

WRINGING THE EMOTIONS

There was a tag line on the cover of one of the confession magazines I used to write for some years ago. It said 'Stories so real they could happen to you'. I think this sums up the essence of good characterisation.

The tag doesn't refer merely to the stories, but to the fictional people involved in them. The problems and dramas of the characters in those stories were designed to strike a chord in every reader who read them. It was the 'There but for the grace of God go I' factor, to quote yet another useful proverb of proven words.

As a reader you may well have known a girl like the one in the story, or the circumstances may even have happened to you. This is the human factor that interweaves with fiction so subtly and smoothly that when it's done well, it's difficult to tell one from the other.

So how can a larger-than-life character such as James Bond or Rhett Butler be anything like the man next door or the bloke stacking shelves at Sainsbury's? The truth is, he's not at all like that, and nor do we really want him to be. We must hold on to our fantasies. We're perfectly well aware that novels are fiction, but for that journey through the pages, we're transported into another world, vicariously sharing whatever twists and turns the author has put the characters through. We become part of their lives.

I'm willing to bet that every woman who ever read a family saga fantasises a little that the hero is sweeping her off her feet at the vital moment; every thriller addict imagines *he's* stepping in the shoes of the intrepid hero who defies all the evil skills of the villain and scales every height imaginable in his quest to bring him to justice. It's harmless role play.

If this reader-character identification doesn't happen to you when you're reading, then you're sadly missing out on everything a writer is aiming for, and you're probably temperamentally unsuited to writing fiction. Fiction, after all, is intended to be both an entertainment and a pseudo wish-fulfilment for the reader, and the writer who is doing her job properly knows that.

It cannot be emphasised enough that to get an emotional impact from your readers, you must be prepared to put plenty of emotion in. Why should your reader feel moved to tears over a scene involving a small child being found drowned if you don't feel totally involved in such a terrible and tragic happening yourself? Be totally involved, and your readers will be involved as well.

With this in mind, I suggest that the two human conditions that produce the best and the worst in us all are being in love and being at war. The next two sections explain more fully how I deal with these conditions in fictional terms.

CHARACTERS IN LOVE

It's not always easy to lose your own sense of embarrassment when writing about people in love, but much depends on the kind of story you're writing.

It may be the kind of gentle romantic novel that doesn't demand too many actual clinches. It may be a short story in which every word must count, so that the emotions of your lovers are only lightly touched. A funny story may still involve tender love scenes, since laughter can be very akin to passion and often leads to it. It may be a powerfully sexy novel, with explicit or frankly torrid writing. None of these methods of describing characters in love is wrong - providing it suits them and their situations.

Whatever kind of characters yours are, they will have created their own kind of aura by the time you get to their love scenes, and your own control over them will dictate the terms of the writing. It would be totally unrealistic to have two strong-willed lovers conducting a passive, euphemistic sort of dialogue, simply because you wrestled with your conscience over the things people say when they're in love. It would be just as unlikely to have a reticent young girl, in an era when things were less permissive than they are now, suddenly coming out with Anglo-Saxon words to demand every refinement in lovemaking from her lover.

The style of your love scenes is dependent on the temperaments of the characters you've created, as well as on the time and setting of their background. Getting it wrong will certainly jar on your readers.

An autocratic historical heroine is hardly going to throw herself into the arms of a gentleman caller. A girl of the nineties out on the town and fancying a guy in a pub probably would. The first would involve lengthier dialogue and the manners of the times while the two got to know one another. The second might well be a raunchy and suggestive scene, with the outcome heavily signposted.

My twenties housemaid character, Amy Moore, in my book *To Love and Honour* (Grafton), was very lacking in self-confidence when the book began, and was intimidated by her much bolder friend. When love suddenly entered her life, she was as much amazed by the fact that a young man could prefer her to the brasher Tess, as she was dazzled by the whole experience. Early in the book Amy and Daniel are in a tea room, with the first intimation that it could be the start of a love affair.

> 'I was supposed to ask you home to tea tomorrow, but now my mother's ill, we'll have to postpone it,' he said regretfully. 'Would you have come, Amy?'
>
> Her face flushed, and he thought he had never seen anything so beautiful. She was transparently lovely, natural, and undoubtedly innocent, not like her friend. Attractive though Tess was, Daniel suspected she was a bit of a tart. For him, Amy had the kind of innocence that was its own protection.
>
> 'I - I think so,' she said dubiously, her glance unconsciously artless, and they both laughed, delighting in the game of flirtation that had hardly begun.
>
> 'But you can't help wondering if I really do have a mother, and if I'm respectable, or if I secretly mean to carry you away to my tent in the desert,' he said dramatically.
>
> Amy giggled. 'Like Rudolph Valentino in *The Sheikh*,' she said. 'Wasn't he simply wonderful?'
>
> 'If you say so. But don't say it too often or I shall get jealous.'
>
> Amy took a sip of tea, watching him from above the rim of her cup. He had lovely dark eyes. He wasn't so unlike Valentino, not as far as she was concerned anyway.
>
> 'Will you really? But he's only an image on the silver screen, and you're right here,' she said before she stopped to think, and blushed scarlet immediately.

The characters' reactions, and the way they fence with one another, are exactly right for them, for the period, and for the mood of the scene. Their world is very much that of the silent film era, and their dialogue reflects their familiarity with it.

All the time I was writing about these characters, I tried to think myself back into that world, to sense how they would behave and react to everything that happened to them. In essence, I wore their shoes, and shared their emotions.

Compare that scene with one much later in the book. They have moved on, grown apart, and, because of circumstances each has married someone else. Although there has been much bitterness between them, love hasn't died. And after a traumatic night during the General Strike, they're alone in Amy's rooms.

```
    'I told the caretaker I was a relative,' he said. 'I
had to be sure you were all right, Amy. I - oh God. I
just couldn't keep away any longer. I've thought about
you all night long, wanting you and cursing everything
that's come between us. I still love you, Amy, you know
that, don't you? You knew it last night -'
    She felt the dryness of a little sob in her throat, and
she was hardly conscious of either of them moving. She
merely seemed to sway towards him, and the next moment
she was in his arms and he had kicked the door shut behind
him, shutting out the rest of the world.
    'We shouldn't be here like this,' she sobbed against his
chest, when she was dazed with his kisses and the passion
that seemed to have burst like a flame between them after
months of repression.
    'Where else should we be?' he demanded, the masculine
aggressor now that her responses had told him everything
he needed to know. Whatever she felt for Bert Figgins,
it was nothing compared to this. Never had been, nor ever
could be.
    She didn't try to deny the unspoken truth of it. She
spoke in a brittle, high voice, as if she had to try to
put everything right at once.
    'Daniel, I'm sorry - for everything. For making such a
mess of things -'
    'Hush, sweetheart. You didn't make a mess of things. It
was - well, it was fate playing with us -'
    Daniel's arms folded around her, and without realising
it, she melted against him.
```

> 'You can trust me, Amy darling. I'd never hurt you.'
> In her thin cotton nightdress and dressing-gown, she became aware of the erratic beating of her heart against his own, and realised how little there was between them. So little keeping them apart ... her head lifted slowly to look into his eyes, and her breath caught.
> 'Oh, my Amy, I want you so much –' the words seemed to be dragged out of him.
> 'And I want you,' she whispered, knowing exactly what he meant, her need soaring to match his own.
> 'Is he here?' He couldn't speak Bert's name now.
> 'No one's here except the caretaker, and he won't disturb us.'
> She was giving her consent and they both knew it. She wanted to feel his body become part of hers, to be whole and alive and in the place where she belonged.

These scenes illustrate the nature of these lovers. They are characters of their time. A girl in the twenties didn't jump lightly into bed with anyone without being desperately afraid and aware of the consequences. In the book, despite everything that's gone before, their love has remained constant, but the restraints of the period are still there. The characters are true to themselves. They have developed from their first tentative flirtation to the fulfilment of their love, even though troubles inevitably still lie ahead.

When two fictional characters who are obviously destined for a love affair have logically entered into a new phase of their relationship, readers will be wanting more. Don't keep them waiting for ever, and don't be a tease. If you've promised them a love scene, however subtly implied, be prepared to give it to them. If you don't, they, like your characters, will probably go off the boil.

CHARACTERS AT WAR

Just as love scenes between characters are an integral part of a love story, battle scenes are as inevitable in a novel involving war. How can it be otherwise? If this is the kind of story in which you place your characters, let them experience the horrors, dangers and tensions to the full.

143

If you skirt around the big events, the traumas, the skirmishes, the blood and gore of it all, you're being less than honest with your readers. And you're missing out on what is a highly imaginative and very visual area of writing.

I didn't know how much I was going to relish putting my characters into battle combat until I actually did so. After all, it's the quintessential conflict. But what did I know about the American Civil War, or the Indian Mutiny, Culloden, the First and Second World Wars, or the Crimean War? The simple answer is very little - apart from the Second World War - yet I've involved very different characters in all of these wars and battles in my various novels. And I gained far more than might be imagined from the mere researching of events and sequential data. I gained an intense insight into the kind of characters who would endure and survive, or go under, or eventually emerge the stronger from the worst possible conditions.

People can endure the most unimaginable tortures. They have their own inner strengths for coping with disaster, and never more so than when you put them in the midst of a terrible battle. They may find reserves of courage they never knew they had, or they may find their terror is unsurmountable. An unlikely hero can emerge out of a desperate situation. A turncoat coward can ruin a carefully planned strike at the enemy. Your characters can lift a battle scene into one of almost superhuman achievements, or they can reduce it to its most pathetic, poignant examination of human frailties.

Never underestimate the power of the characters when you put them into any well-documented data such as the Battle of the Somme or Vietnam. Clashes of personality will always develop in such fictional dramas. Partnerships will be forged, perhaps only for the briefest time; but they will have significant effects on the participants. A strange kind of love/hate can develop between characters thrown together for a period of time, especially in confinement, whether it be in a concentration camp, a mud-filled trench, a flimsy aeroplane, or the claustrophobic atmosphere of a submarine.

Wherever you put such characters together, giving them a common goal to fight, or a common resentment, a special relationship will develop between them. Their strengths and their vulnerabilities will emerge. In the midst of horror and death you can bring your characters very much to life.

This is not the time to be reticent with the dialogue of a ruthless terrorist with a deadly task of wholesale slaughter in mind. He will be a terse, aggressive, blasphemous, cold-blooded killer. He will move stealthily, with the utmost care and deliberation. The tension in his make-up as he builds up to his allotted task will be almost painfully apparent, and everything you say about him will leave your readers in no doubt that he's the kind of man who enjoys killing, and feels no remorse at his victims' fate. Putting yourself in his shoes is uncomfortable at the very least.

When you decide to write a story involving a battle, the scope of characters is enormous, from the conscientious objector fighting his own personal battles to the half-crazed psychopath with a killer instinct who dons a uniform for his own ends. You may write about the giant of a commander who knows he has a job to do, and wants to get his boys back home safely; or the rookie, who goes into battle with a St Christopher around his neck and terror in his heart.

Apart from professional servicemen, most of the characters you put into battle will have come from very different backgrounds. The grocer who has joined up in a wave of patriotism; the nurse who only wanted to see the world; the group of kids joining up for a dare and finding that real war is very different from the Hollywood version; the brothers, fathers, sweethearts, husbands and lovers, poignantly far away from home on important anniversaries; the college friends joining the Wrens together for a lark ... From then on, how each of these people faces up to their new lives is up to you.

Never waste the potential of such rich characters by giving them less than they deserve in their death struggles and their triumphs. The need to survive must become paramount. The choice of words you use must be strong, emotive and visual.

In my novel *Scarlet Rebel* (Severn House), I freely broke my own rule of not naming characters with the same initials. No rule is inflexible, and John Joyner Innes was the name of my Scottish grandfather. The inclusion of a purely fictional character using his name was a personal indulgence. In the scene below, the Battle of Culloden is taking its lethal toll of the Highlanders. My hero, Jamie Mackinnon, is the narrator.

God knew how many he had killed or maimed. He was past caring. It would go down in his record in heaven or hell for this day. He suddenly heard the roaring voice of John Joyner Innes nearby, cursing and blaspheming into battle. The sheer sight of him, kilt swirling, his huge girth, murder in his face, was enough to make an entire army quail. But not this army. Not Cumberland's men.

'Get the bastards, John Joyner!' Jamie heard himself screaming. Cannon fire was exploding all around him, rocking his senses and making wool of his brains. An arm, severed from its owner, touched his face as it was blown to the ground. He trod on it without noticing the soft dead flesh or the oozing blood! He was crazed.

'I'll save a few for ye, laddie!' John Joyner bellowed back at him, and then the bellowing dwindled to a horrific gurgling as the spattering of grapeshot caught him full in the wide expanse of his belly, and blood spurted out as if from a flour sprinkler. He dropped like a boulder, and Jamie knelt without thought behind the great mound of his body to fire straight up into the next leaping redcoat's heart.

The soldier fell soundlessly, right over the dead body of his erstwhile friend, and toppled onto Jamie. Then he knew sheer horror as blood gushed from the soldier's mouth and the great hole in his red jacket. What was uniform and what was blood, or were they all one and the same? The wildness of the thoughts sped in and out of his mind as though they went through a sieve. He pushed with all his strength to get the body away from him, but there was always another, and another ...

CHAPTER 11

CHILDREN'S FICTIONAL CHARACTERS

REACHING A YOUNGER AUDIENCE
THE PRECOCIOUS NARRATOR
ANIMAL CHARACTERS
ENTER THE DRAGON
INANIMATE CHARACTERS

CHAPTER 11

REACHING A YOUNGER AUDIENCE

Writers need readers, and most adult readers had a love of reading instilled in them when they were very young. The pleasure of 'reading', when loosely interpreted as fantasising in the magic of a story, can begin in a child of a few months of age.

I know this from personal experience. I used to show my children picture books, explaining the pictures in simple terms, long before they learned to speak, let alone understand what reading meant, and I saw the interest and enthusiasm with which they devoured such sessions. An interest in stories that's begun when a child is very young will never leave them, and will be a source of pleasure and enjoyment all their lives.

A person who has a book to read is never alone, for he has all the wonderful characters he discovers within the pages with whom to share his quiet hours.

There could probably be no greater contrast in creating the kind of characters involved in the most intense adult situations in the last chapter - those of love and war - and creating characters for children's reading pleasure. But you should never underestimate your audience. Apart from the tinies, who would naturally prefer safe, cuddly topics to read about, older children adore reading about spooks and witches. It's a well-known fact that children have a strange enjoyment of being frightened - just so long as the goodies eventually overcome the baddies, with the comforting sense that good triumphs over evil remaining the constant.

There's something of that childlike wish for the perfect Nirvana in all of us. Why else does pantomime still flourish so magnificently in our cynical world? We yell and hiss at the wicked villain; we laugh with the impossibly grotesque Dame - usually played by a man and we cheer on the valiant hero, played usually by a woman dressed as a boy. Where pantomime is concerned, there was never a truer proverb than 'There's nowt so queer as folk'! Children easily accept all this, partly because of the group sensation of security, I suspect, and partly because it can so obviously be seen to be play-acting. But they can be canny readers. They will spot a flaw in a character in a story and are less prepared to forgive it than an adult.

You can't get away with anything in your writing, and neither should you dream of 'writing down' to a younger age group; this is totally unacceptable.

Having said that, younger readers obviously don't have the patience or concentration of older readers. They won't be bothered to pursue a scene or a chapter which may explain in depth something that has gone before, delaying the action. What they want is to experience that action, they want honesty and clarity, and they want it *now*.

You need to know your potential readers, and there's no better way than getting to know how they tick than by listening to them. Listen to their chatter when they pour out of schools at the end of the day. It's a revelation. The tinies will be wanting to tell Mum all that they've done that day, and will be in rose-coloured raptures about their school-teacher, the undoubted new heroine in their lives. Slightly older ones may be reluctant to tear themselves away from the side of their Best Friend, the new, important person in their lives.

The next age group may be chattering about school sporting activities, or homework, or of their resentment against a teacher or the class bully, or the prospect of school trips. Teenagers will be beyond all this, except for school trips, especially those taking them abroad. School activities, if mentioned at all, will be quickly dismissed. Teenagers now have newer and more interesting horizons; the opposite sex; make-up for girls; football matches and motorbikes for boys; peer groups and clubs; pseudo-adult activities; part-time jobs; money.

Of course, this is a very generalised scenario, but it does present a picture of the varied diversions of your potential readers. Listening to them can be a good way of finding out where their interests lie. It's a fact of life that far too many of us never listen to our children properly. The Americans even promoted a special theme on the subject, with car stickers and badges, asking 'When did you last listen to your kids?' It may be brash, but it makes a point.

And if you think you're alone in listening in on children's conversations and observing their lifestyles for fictional purposes, you have a very good predecessor. Charles Dickens visited Bowes Academy in Yorkshire, at that time a school for so-called difficult and unwanted children in order to see for himself the appalling things that went on in the guise of caring. The result was the heinous character of Mr Squeers, the sadistic headmaster of Dotheboys Hall in *Nicholas Nickleby*.

Many more ideas and interests than the ones I listed above can be explained when you create your children's characters, depending on the age group you're writing for. It's not the purpose of this book to go into the mechanics of that specialised genre. For that, I recommend Tessa Krailing's *How to Write for Children*. I merely offer suggestions as to some of the imaginative characters you can create for their reading pleasure.

THE PRECOCIOUS NARRATOR

There are many types of fictional characters that would appeal to children. I want to offer only a sample. To my mind, high on the list must come the precocious narrator, animal characters and inanimate characters. I will leave any other types to your imagination.

At some time in our lives, we've probably all met the child whose attitudes or conversations really stick in our gullets and make us cringe. They come in all shapes, sizes and ages. They can be the bane of our lives, but when you fictionalise them, they make marvellous characters to write about. Imagine the ghastly kid along the way who's such a know-it-all; the school bully who terrorises everyone he comes into contact with; the bumptious ten-year-old, going on 35; the pre-teen with the passable singing voice who thinks she's the next Madonna; the leader of the gang, who's there only because everybody else is afraid to challenge him; the over-polite, over-sweetly-behaved child everyone except her doting mother loves to hate; the slightly disabled child who is cashing in on his disability to make everyone around him cater to his every whim; the child-genius, sickeningly aware of his talent.

Any of these, in fictional terms, would make a powerful main character. And working out why, and how, he perpetrates his particular artistry would in itself be an interesting exercise in child psychology. The children's author Phyllis A Whitney suggests that our adult faults had their beginnings when we were children. I find this an interesting comment, even though I'm not altogether convinced by it, and I think it's too narrow a focus to pin *all* future failings on childhood. But it's certainly an idea that can be incorporated in the whys and wherefores of fictional characters behaving in the way they do.

All the attributes you apply to creating characters in adult fiction can be applied to children's characters. In that respect, there's little difference. Characters must have motivation for all that they do. They must have their own voices, their own personalities, their faults and their virtues.

But the way children in stories project themselves will be different. They have none of the inhibitions we develop as we grow older. If something annoys a small child, he will say so at once, no matter who is listening, to many parents' embarrassment. Children can also be very cruel, both towards each other and about each other.

These are the kind of things to remember when you choose to use a child narrator. And of course, the language they use will be different. Smaller children simply don't have the vocabulary of older ones, and certainly not that of adults. So to give a child aged five a string of long words that would be totally beyond him to say is stretching the incredulity of your similarly aged reader to breaking point. In fact, you'd have lost her long ago, because she wouldn't understand the words either, and would be bored, frustrated or uninterested in your story, no matter how wonderful it might have been until that moment when she heard the characters speak.

It's said that children's fiction can be broadly separated into two main categories, that involving realism and that involving fantasy. Realism would obviously involve the precocious characters we would love to hate, and whom we would be willing on towards their just desserts. It would also include the many pseudo-heroic or comical deeds of characters like *Just William, The Railway Children,* all the characters in the Enid Blyton adventure stories, or the more homespun adventures of *Anne of Green Gables.* In all these cases, children would readily be able to identify with the fictional characters. They would recognise something in themselves, or in their contemporaries.

It all comes down to that good old reader-identification again. And in all the examples given above, one central character takes on the role of being larger than life, whether by being precocious, or being a survivor, or just being good leadership material. There's not so much difference in the variety of role play between the characters in children's stories and those in adult ones. The only difference is in the games they play.

At a children's-fiction workshop I attended, one of the exercises we were given was to write down everything we could think of to do with a childhood fear. The object was to expand our minds into thinking of everything that might be portrayed in a character in a story involving that particular fear. My choice was fear of the dark. The list had to be written in a given time of five minutes. No frills were expected from the students, just random thoughts that entered the mind about the subject. My list is given below.

Fear of the Dark

Claustrophobia. Disorientation. Hearing small sounds magnified in the dark. Scratchings, creepings. Doors opening, closing, creaking, banging. Being shut in a cupboard. Lights failing. Blackness. Fear of being blind. Fear of the unknown. Being buried alive. Coffins. Churchyards. Eerie sounds. Fear of ghosts, demons, devils. Being crushed. Heart pounding. Unable to breathe. Listening for every sound. Unable to speak/scream. Throat drying up. Throat aching with fear. Desperate need for the toilet. Stomach boiling. Sweating. Burrowing beneath the bedclothes. Clutching anything familiar, teddy bear/doll/blanket. Searching for a light switch. Touching something that could be a hand/ a face/ an animal. Cold. Clammy. Hearing someone/ something else breathing. Hearing strange voices or hearing laughter/soft/loud/creepy. Imagination working overtime. Everything unreal. Faint shadows becoming monsters. Feeling weightless. Afraid to move forward or back. Having something unidentifiable touch you. Fear that you'll die alone/that no one will ever find you. Loneliness. Wanting parents/friends/anyone. Panic. Strange, unidentified smells. Moonless, starless. Night. Incense. Rituals. Midnight. Witches, Broomsticks. Mystery. Confusion. Eclipse. Falling. Impenetrable blackness. Hell.

Phew. I don't imagine any writer would put *all* those impressions into one character in a children's story, but it should give you an idea of the way your mind can encompass a mass of images from a given idea in a given time. It was also interesting to note at this workshop, how many of the other students were nodding as each of us took our turn in reading out the images evoked by our own particular 'childhood fear'. We could all identify with a single theme.

ANIMAL CHARACTERS

Proven favourites among children that come into the fantasy world of fiction are animal characters who take on human personalities.

A child has a natural fear of animals, partly because of adult intervention in not wanting a baby to be touched by a cat or dog, for obvious reasons, and partly because most animals are so much larger than the small child.

Even if they're not, the simple fact that they're not like us, that they have four legs, coarse hair or fur covering their bodies, that they wriggle or jump or scratch, makes them alien beings as far as a child is concerned. Reducing the child's fear of animals by putting them in human form has the effect of diminishing some of that fear, though it can also have an adverse effect, when the seemingly innocent figure in human form suddenly reveals his true identify, as does the wolf in *Little Red Riding Hood*.

Many of the stories that have stood the test of time, and yet can have children almost shivering beneath the covers with a mixture of fear and delight as a parent reads the bedtime story, are those involving animal characters interwoven with fictional children. In such fairytales as *Little Red Riding Hood* and *Goldilocks*, the central character is human and under considerable stress. Not the kind of thing you might imagine a child needs to be told about at bedtime! Yet 'bedtime stories' are exactly how they are described, and a child who hears the same story, told again and again and obviously with its 'happy ending', will lose the initial fear, and the characters will breed their own familiarity.

Children are quickly able to identify with such animal characters when they have human connections, which is probably the real secret of creating them successfully. *The Wind in the Willows* was a marvellous pot pourri of such characters. Children have such receptive imaginations, and readily accept that such transformations can happen, even if only in books and comics and magazines. Some of their own inventive writings are pure, uncluttered inspiration and are well worth reading in any classroom. The way children themselves view their favourite fictional characters, and those that they create themselves, is the way we should be creating them.

Instant pictures come to mind at the very mention of Mickey Mouse and all his friends; Tom and Jerry; Rupert the Bear; Kermit the Frog and Miss Piggy; Sooty and Sweep. All are well-loved animal characters, and there are many more. There's no reason why any animal you choose can't be fictionalised in a way to make them equally loveable to children.

One of my daughters had a story, called *The Lonely Pony*, published in a magazine when she was only eleven years old. It was a short, simple story with a sympathetic main character, but perfectly suited to the needs of that particular magazine and its readership. The obvious message is to study your markets.

ENTER THE DRAGON

One of my children's favourite fictional characters was the dragon. Did he ever really exist, or is he the stuff of myths and legends? And does it really matter, when it comes to the wealth of fiction written about him, from the courageous exploits of St George to slay him, to comic cartoon dragon characters? He has long been a stalwart in children's fiction, and will probably never go out of fashion.

Imagine that you have decided to depict a dragon as your main character in a story. The first thing to remember is that he's been done many times before, so you would need to think up a fresh and original idea to make it a viable proposition for publication. With this in mind, it's a very good idea to write down everything you can think of regarding this creature and his world to see where your thoughts lead you. Just as you wrote out your checklist for a specific character in an adult story, so your particular dragon needs to have a definite personality that is unique to him. In fact, this was another of the exercises included at the children's fiction workshop I attended. My list of everything that might be involved in a dragon's world is as follows, exactly as I thought of it in the five minutes for this exercise. Again, in this short time, no details were expected, just words and phrases written down as the ideas and images occurred.

Dragons

Breathing fire. Fire gone out. A thin blue flame. Magic. Sorcerers. Magic charms. Strength, power, size. Scaly skin, shiny bright or dulled by having a bad cold. Colour faded from scales. Roaring voice/squeaking voice. Wizards and witches. Castles. Moats. Transylvania. Rescuing damsels in distress. Mythical creatures. Fear. Spells. Potions. A modern dragon. A historical dragon. A dragon in a time-warp. A dragon let loose in Hyde Park. A dragon at the zoo. A friendly dragon. A soft-hearted dragon. A cartoon dragon. A fantasy world of dragons. A dragon at school. A flying dragon. A cowardly dragon. A dragon with no tail. A baby dragon. Dragons in space. A sea-sick dragon. A pet dragon. A dragon in the bath. A talking/chatterbox dragon. A computer-whiz dragon. A dragon with toothache/ earache (do dragons have ears?) or a headache. The smallest dragon. A dragon scared of fire. A bad-tempered dragon. A disappearing dragon. A hypochondriac dragon. A dragon with a chesty cough. A dragon with a fear of people/mice. An orphan dragon.

You'll see that, in this case, after the first set of more imaginative words I came up with, my own thoughts developed into a list of what could have been prospective story titles or the briefest of character descriptions, any of which could have produced a story involving a different kind of dragon character. Other people at the workshop produced many different interpretations of this simple exercise, some with far more colourful and intriguing situations than mine.

I don't profess to be a children's author, apart from writing a few magazine stories for children and half a dozen or so teenage novels. But anyone with an imagination should be able to create a list of similar ideas about a particular emotion such as fear of the dark, or a fictional character such as the well-worn dragon, giving him a new slant.

INANIMATE CHARACTERS

Just like the Daleks in *Doctor Who*, and the space fantasy figures created for adults, inanimate characters have a piquant appeal for children. Dolls, teddy bears and other toys apparently coming to life are the obvious.

And it hardly needs to be said which have been the most successful inanimate fictional characters in recent years. *Thomas the Tank Engine* and friends must come very high on the list. I doubt that the Revd W Awdry, creator of Thomas and his friends, knew what incredible success lay ahead of him when he wrote the first simple story involving an engine with a face and a voice and a personality. And surely, therein lies the secret of humanising the inanimate - a face, a voice and a personality. We see him, we hear him and we like him. Or dislike him, as the case may be.

That which makes inanimate characters so very accessible to children's imaginations lies in giving them human needs, emotions and failings, in the same way these things were bestowed on the animal characters. I'm not sure into which category the Teenage Mutant Ninja Turtles should be entered, since they seem to be somewhere between the two. Whatever your feelings on them, they became an instant success with children, and children, after all, are the experts. If they don't like a character, you've wasted your time creating him.

The Mister Men were endearing fictional creatures with no particular substance as far as I could see. They were just cartoon figures, each with a human failing, and a story to tell explaining this failing and how it could be improved - Mister Small, Mister Thin, Mister Clever, Mister Greedy and so on. And all of them reached their audience, because they were so readily identifiable.

Who would have thought the Flowerpot Men would have become such cult figures? Unintelligible, talking gibberish, but always friendly in an oddly cuddly way, and with their own version of the confidante character in Little Weed. How could two puppets jigging about in flowerpots ever have become so real? And yet, for all of us bringing up our children in the early days of children's television, they did.

The House That Sneezed by David Lennie had as its main character a house that planned to get rid of its dirty and untidy occupants by devious and clever means. A simple idea, but one that would definitely appeal to children while delivering a simple and unmoralised message. Who could ever forget the delicious and loveable Herbie, the car that drove itself and frequently did its own thing? And this idea was brought right up to date through sophistication and computerisation by *Knight Rider.*

The Wizard of Oz combined a mixture of animal and inanimate characters to accompany Dorothy along the yellow brick road. The Tin Man wanted a heart. The Scarecrow wanted some brains. The Lion wanted some courage. And didn't we love them all, and will them on to achieve their dearest wishes?

Any familiar object could be humanised to make it an interesting character for children's fiction. Look around you, and see what would animate successfully. Apart from the flowerpots in *The Flowerpot Men,* what about actual garden tools? Their appearances lend themselves to the kind of characters they could become. A racy electric mower; a haughty rake; a demure hand trowel; a bossy spade; a fastidious fork; a snivelling sieve.

Think about everyday kitchen equipment too. The run-away vacuum cleaner; the heavyweight iron; the singing kettle; the snooty teapot. And the lazy clock - think of all the various implications that could have for its owner. Toothbrushes and toothpaste; dancing milk bottles; 'talking' potatoes, carrots and other vegetables - the influence of TV advertising inanimates could play a large part in getting your imaginative juices going.

The precedent in apparel is surely *The Red Shoes* which had a life of their own; the book is both a classic story and a ballet, but the basic idea of animated clothing could be put to use in creating other characters. The wellington boots with military aspirations; the cowboy hat that wanted to go to Texas; the umbrella that hated to get wet.

If ever there was scope for letting adult imaginations run riot, it must surely be in the realms of children's fantasy fiction. But always keep in mind that no matter how fantastic your characters and plot, the end of the story must always justify the beginning. Children, like adults, will expect logical solutions to all the problems their protagonists encounter, and that's no easy task. But if you can do it, children's characters can be a delight to read about and a delight to create, perhaps because there's still something of the child in all of us.

CHAPTER 12

SUMMARY

KNOWING AND UNDERSTANDING
YOUR CHARACTERS
TESTING THE STRENGTH OF YOUR
CHARACTERS
THE FINAL CHECKLIST
LETTING THEM GO

CHAPTER 12

KNOWING AND UNDERSTANDING
YOUR CHARACTERS

One of the most rewarding things anyone can say to a fiction writer is how much they enjoyed their story. We all want to hear such a compliment, and we wouldn't be human if it didn't make us preen a little. But if the compliment goes a little deeper, then it's praise indeed.

What I'm referring to is hearing that your readers understood, sympathised with, cringed at, loathed, fell in love with, or were able to laugh or cry with, your characters. Not all at the same time of course, nor about the same character!

It's a great thrill to any author to hear how much a reader adored her Vanessa, say, or hated her Sebastian. It's the knowledge of having brought those characters so much into focus, so much to real, vibrant life that readers shared all their emotions. It's very gratifying that they felt they knew the characters well enough to quote them by name and to remark on their appearances, their failings and their triumphs. When that happens, then you really know you've succeeded in what you set out to do.

Once you've got the characters right, and have got them crystal clear in your own mind as to their aspirations and their motivations, then the plot, while obviously demanding a lot of concentrated work on your behalf, will nevertheless take on its own unique shape more easily. Characters that live and breathe in your own mind will all the more clearly show you the way they want to go in any situation you devise for them.

I sincerely believe that you must be prepared to love all the characters you create. With some of them, this is a very easy thing to do, especially those that are instantly and obviously destined to be attractive people. The beautiful heroine and the dashing hero in a romance; the flamboyant sea captain; even the helpless, bumbling hijacker getting everything wrong will nevertheless have his soft, sympathy-drawing side. We have no difficulty loving such creations as the children's loveable animal character or the blazing gun-toting sheriff, larger than life, saving entire communities by his heroism.

But what of the rest? The anti-heroes, the wicked stepmothers, the villains, the murderers? This is where, as a writer, you must become both totally involved and quite dispassionate. You mentally divide yourself in two. The practical side of you will see all the potential in these strong characters, and you will describe them with all the vigour you can manage. If they are meant to be evil, then you must make them as evil as you can, with no holds barred. Your sole intention is to make your readers hate them as much as they deserve to be hated for the wrong-doers that they are. In that sense, you will obviously hate them too.

But the other side of you, the creative side, must also have a strange fondness for these creations of yours, seeing and understanding the weaknesses in their characters that maybe only you know in your heart. Just as a mother loves all her brood, however much they go astray, so you should care for all your characters. If they are important enough to be included in your story and have a real purpose for being there, then the worst evil-doers are every bit as deserving of your care and attention as the good guys.

TESTING THE STRENGTH OF YOUR CHARACTERS

Revising their work is something about which authors have mixed feelings. I've already said that I don't believe in too much alteration if everything looks good as it is. It's not always easy, but you should try to be as objective as you can when you assess what you've written. I believe in being selective in revision, especially when it comes to changing specifics about my characters. It's all too easy to change an adverb or a phrase just for the sake of it, without really considering that the new words give a completely different impression from the one that was so definite in your mind in the first place.

Without realising it, you can subtly alter the impression you're making about your character, so that she is no longer as clear-cut as she was in the beginning. And if she is wrongly altered for you, she will be wrongly altered for your reader. Proceed with caution as far as revising every word and phrase is concerned.

But testing the strength and consistency of your characters is certainly where revision is necessary, and very valuable. There are vital questions you should ask yourself, and if the answers don't come up to scratch, it's definitely time for more revision.

Some of the following questions may seem unnecessary when applied to your particular writing. You may think you would never make such simple errors as the ones implied by the questions. I assure you that despite the number of short stories and novels I have had published, the need for such watchfulness still applies to me. No one is word-perfect, the first time around. And it's amazing how often the simplest flaws fail to come under our scrutiny in the heat of the writing, and need to be rechecked before you send your story off to an editor. Even if you fail to spot the inaccuracies yourself, you can be pretty sure the editor will find them.

I find it pays to detail things in lists. Perhaps this can be called a shopping-list mentality, but following my lists helps me to keep everything organised in my mind. It may help you too. So, with no apologies, I offer yet another checklist of how you might be testing the strength and consistency of your own fictional characters, and acting on your final revisions, before you send your best work to your chosen publisher.

THE FINAL CHECKLIST

- Do your characters live up to the names you've chosen for them?
- Are there too many similar-sounding names in your story, so that readers will become confused?
- Have you muddled your short story by using too many characters?
- Have you used too much dialect in the dialogue, instead of just instilling the flavour of regional accents, for instance?
- Has your character's dialogue/tone of voice undergone radical changes without logical motivation?
- Have you loaded your dialogue with too many adverbs/not enough adverbs/inaccurate ones?
- Does the dialogue move the story forward?
- Does the dialogue perform its function of giving information to the other characters, and to the readers?
- Is the dialogue ultra trite, holding up the story and just padding out the pages?
- Do your characters have the same colour eyes/hair and other physical attributes or peculiarities at the end of the story as they did at the beginning, and are they consistent throughout?
- Are their mannerisms the same throughout, or have you changed them slightly as you progressed through the story? If so, is this feasible and able to be accepted readily by readers?
- Would you be as attracted to your heroine/hero as you expect your hero/heroine to be?
- Have you changed your character's height/weight/posture during the story?
- If so, is it relevant to change their age because of the time span of the story?
- Have your characters 'aged' logically during a long time span?
- Are the descriptions of your characters as visual as possible?
- Have you gone off at a tangent and given a character an entirely different motivation from the original one?
- Have you changed the hero halfway through a romance, when the reader was confidently expecting the heroine to end up with the original one?

- Does your super-sleuth seem too far-fetched to be true, solving everything by seemingly magical and unexplained processes?
- Do your characters' material trappings/cars/jewellery/houses, etc., reflect their financial status, personalities and lifestyles?
- Is your heroine as real to you as your best friend?
- Is your hero as real to you as your husband/sweetheart/lover?
- Are your love scenes as romantic as possible, avoiding outdated clichés and anything that might attract ridicule?
- Do your characters seem to live in a vacuum, without a past?
- Have you given them logical hope for a future?
- Have you checked all relevant and up-to-date facts regarding military/police procedures or other relevant occupations/careers, such as nursing?
- Have you disposed of your villains as sensibly and/or gruesomely as readers would expect?
- Have you been careful and consistent regarding view-point?
- Is there sufficient conflict and tension between the characters in your story to keep your readers interested?
- Do you feel that if the characters in your story walked through your living-room door, you would know them instantly?
- Have you really cared about your characters and what happens to them?

LETTING THEM GO

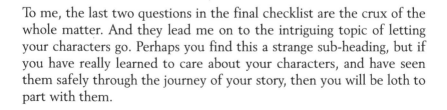

To me, the last two questions in the final checklist are the crux of the whole matter. And they lead me on to the intriguing topic of letting your characters go. Perhaps you find this a strange sub-heading, but if you have really learned to care about your characters, and have seen them safely through the journey of your story, then you will be loth to part with them.

It will have been a simple matter to let go of your walk-ons. They flitted in and out of your story and played their shadowy part. The minor ones, the subsidiaries, and the confidantes may or may not be there at the final showdown scenes in your story. The central characters most certainly will be. And sometimes you will feel hard put to know just how to end their story.

It's not my purpose here to offer advice on writing final scenes and winding up your story, only to comment on how you will feel at parting from your characters. Because if you have defined them well, then in the midst of your joy at actually finishing your story, you will feel the same sense of regret you would feel at parting from old friends.

At least, you should do. If you don't, then perhaps they are still not as real to you as they should be. I feel very strongly that it's a good thing to feel this sense of regret at losing the fictional people you have become attached to, having seen them through their good times as well as their bad ones.

You will have rejoiced when they fell in love, married, and had babies. You will have cheered on the next generation at their sports days and their graduations. You will have felt pride in their achievements, whether in the primary school play or in attaining an Honours degree at university.

You will have given your plodding detective all the attributes to make him a full-blown hero in the eyes of his fellows; willed on the wicked villain to be caught and suitably punished, the terrorist to be gunned down as cruelly as he slaughtered his victims; hoped for the entrepreneur to succeed.

Until the end of your story, these people have been totally yours, to do with what you will. And now you and they have to part company.

Stripping it all down to the brutal truth, the characters created out of an author's imagination are no more than words on paper. But to you, the author, they were real people. And to your readers, for whatever length of time they were absorbed in your story, they will be real.

So if you can honestly say that the characters in your story lived up to their potential, and did all that was asked of them, your regret at parting from them will be short-lived. If you've achieved all that you set out to do, you should be feeling a sense of pride in finally being able to let them go. And the best of it is, they're not gone for ever. You only have to turn the pages of your published short story or novel, and they can be instantly back with you again, part of your life again. Aren't we, as authors, the lucky ones!

I'm willing to bet that once you've known the exhilaration of bringing your characters to their happy, satisfactory, thought-provoking or hopeful conclusion, there will probably be a new set all ready and waiting to burst out of that fertile imagination of yours. The pleasure of creating fictional characters becomes addictive, but it is surely one of the most rewarding and exciting of addictions. I wish you much joy in all the characters you create out of your own imagination, skill and talent.

INFORMATION

Writers' Bookshop publishes useful books for new and
established writers alike.

THE CRAFT OF WRITING ROMANCE Jean Saunders
HOW TO WRITE REALISTIC DIALOGUE Jean Saunders
POETRY: HOW TO GET PUBLISHED, HOW TO GET PAID Kenneth C Steven
POET'S HANDBOOK: A GUIDE TO BUILDING BETTER POEMS
Kenneth C Steven
SUCCESSFUL WRITING Teresa McCuaig
HOW TO WRITE NON-FICTION BOOKS Gordon Wells
HOW TO WRITE & SELL A BOOK PROPOSAL Stella Whitelaw
THE MAGAZINE WRITERS' HANDBOOK (9TH EDITION)
Chriss McCallum & Gordon Wells
WRITING ... IS FUN! Gordon Wells
DRAWING ... IS FUN! Susie Hodge

For more information or to order any of these titles,
please get in touch.

Writers' Bookshop

Remus House, Coltsfoot Drive, Peterborough PE2 9JX
Tel 01733 898105 Email info@forwardpress.co.uk
Visit our website www.forwardpress.co.uk